SELLING THE INTANGIBLE

Turn Your Knowledge into Income.
Generate Predictable Profits.
Build a Wildly Successful Digital Product Business.

MEERA KOTHAND

WWW.MEERAKOTHAND.COM

COPYRIGHT © 2021

All rights reserved. No part of this publication may be reproduced, distributed, stored in a retrieval system, or transmitted in any form or by any means, including photocopying, recording, or other electronic or mechanical methods, without the prior written permission of the author, except by reviewers who may quote brief passages in a review.

For permission requests, please email **meera@meerakothand.com**

SELLING THE INTANGIBLE

TURN YOUR KNOWLEDGE INTO INCOME.
GENERATE PREDICTABLE PROFITS.
BUILD A WILDLY SUCCESSFUL DIGITAL
PRODUCT BUSINESS.

CONTENTS PAGE

INTRODUCTION

THE BIG, BOLD PROMISE 1

ASSUMPTIONS THAT PARALYZE YOUR
FORAY INTO DIGITAL PRODUCTS 7

**SECTION I: UNCOVERING YOUR STRATEGY –
PREPARING FOR EXPLOSIVE
GROWTH 19**

CHAPTER 1: OFFER & SUCCESS STACKING 20

CHAPTER 2: STAGE IDENTIFICATION 37

CHAPTER 3: JOURNEY MAPPING 39

**SECTION II: THE ESSENTIAL DIGITAL PRODUCT
KIT – ORGANIZING & BUILDING
YOUR PRODUCT FOR SUCCESS....55**

CHAPTER 4: WHY PEOPLE DON'T BUY
YOUR STUFF 57

CHAPTER 5: FROM SKELETON TO FLESH 70

CHAPTER 6: OUTSTANDING SALES PAGES 75

CHAPTER 7: PERFECT PRICING 81

CHAPTER 8: LAUNCHING YOUR PRODUCT IN TODAY'S ONLINE SPACE 87

CHAPTER 9: SECRETS TO SCALING YOUR OFFER 103

CHAPTER 10: TOOLS 110

SECTION III: BUILDING YOUR DIGITAL PRODUCT BUSINESS – HOW TO 10× PRODUCTIVITY & PROFITS . 115

CHAPTER 11: YOUR FIRST OR NEXT DIGITAL PRODUCT CAMPAIGN 117

CHAPTER 12: SYSTEMS TO RUN IT LIKE A WELL-OILED MACHINE 130

CHAPTER 13: PRINCIPLES OF EXTRAORDINARY DIGITAL PRODUCT CREATORS 135

CONCLUSION 146

RESOURCES 154

INTRODUCTION
THE BIG, BOLD PROMISE

How in the world are they making $30,000 a month selling e-books and courses?

That was the question that started it all for me.

I didn't know much about digital marketing, but I was fascinated by the idea of cultivating an audience and creating digital customers by turning my knowledge into income.

I've since gone on to build a business primarily from digital products—from simple templates to courses to self-published e-books to memberships.

But nothing about it was easy.

I made mistakes. *A lot* of mistakes.

I never did get my *$1,000 in 30 days* or *5 figures in 6 months,* which made me believe for the longest time that I was the biggest loser around.

I've been irked, disturbed, and frustrated by the assumptions, false yardsticks, and misinformation being spread over and over again about digital products.

Heck, I've even at some point believed some of them myself!

Maybe you're still deciding if digital products are for you. You just want to scratch that itch—can I really make money from digital products—but you're completely new and overwhelmed.

Where do you begin? What are the right actions to take? In what order?

Maybe you already have one or more digital products and are wondering what your next step should be.

Maybe you've hustled and failed. You've read the books and taken the courses but find yourself back at square one every single time.

No matter what your situation, I want you to know that *I see you*.

I know what it's like to wonder if you're the only one not getting it or not doing the right things.

To feel like you're not moving at all no matter how hard you're trying.

I know how it feels to be plagued with doubts.

Creating and launching something as intangible as a digital product can give rise to its own unique set of complexities.

It can also be overwhelming and exhausting when you don't know what to focus on.

Yet, here I am championing digital products.

Why?

Because the beauty of digital products is that you're not just selling your knowledge for income. You're not just teaching people about fitness, Facebook ads, homeschooling, or whatever you teach in your niche.

You're teaching an *entire* way of doing things.

A creator whose work I adored several years back when I was finding resources for my then one-year-old daughter reached out to me recently to tell me that she had bought my course and that it had transformed the way she thought about her business. That was a full-circle moment for me. It was a reminder of the impact and transformation that digital products can provide.

Finding a digital product that solves a nagging pain point can create an enormous sense of satisfaction and change to the way you do things. This feeling isn't limited to just purchases like gadgets or cars, but it can arise from purchases like digital products as well.

THE CASE FOR DIGITAL PRODUCTS & THIS BOOK

The stats from the e-learning market continue to blow expectations completely out of the water.

The worldwide e-learning market is projected to be worth $325 billion in 2025. The US e-learning market could grow by $12.81 billion between 2020 and 2024.[1]

Most books and courses on digital products and course creation sell you on this and jump straight into how you can uncover the perfect niche and presell your product.

Yes, you want to take a bite of this gold-dusted pie and you should! But a critical element skipped in the process is strategy.

You're not just building a product.

You're building a brand asset.

Something that's going to fuel your audience's transformation and journey with your brand.

So the conversation shouldn't start with *"What product (or course) should I create?"* It should start with *"What's my vision for this business model?"*

When you don't set clear intentions at the start of your journey, you'll veer off course from where you intended to go in the first place.

Before we dive into how you can chart your very own plan, let's challenge some of these false "truths" or yardsticks that you perhaps have been believing about digital products.

ASSUMPTIONS THAT PARALYZE YOUR FORAY INTO DIGITAL PRODUCTS

ASSUMPTION 1: ONE DIGITAL PRODUCT WILL CHANGE YOUR LIFE

I love digital products and am very grateful for being able to build the business that I have on them.

But if you're planning on replacing your full-time income solely with digital products in the first three to six months that you're in business, you'll be disappointed.

There are a lot of people who'll tell you that a single course or one main offer is what you'll need to change your life.

You may have heard stories of so-and-so replacing their full-time income with a single product launch.

You're led to believe that everyone has huge six-figure launches every time they create and launch a digital product. Or that you can easily enroll three hundred members in the beta round of your membership launch. Or that one digital product will create a defining moment in your business.

That's simply not true!

I can assure you that these stories are an anomaly, not the norm.

When I started out in 2016, the rule of thumb was *"you just need to sell ten spots in a $97 program."*

About four years later, the rhetoric was *"sell ten spots of a $1,000 program."*

I'm not saying it's impossible. But it's not as easy as putting together a bunch of emails, sending them out to your list, and raking in cash. The online environment is terribly different today.[2]

If you need to make money NOW and you're new to the online space, the last thing I'd recommend is creating a course or a membership.

Surprised, considering this is a book about digital products?

Courses and memberships are incredible revenue streams. I have both of these revenue streams in my own business model, but they do take time.

They're not magic bullets.

This doesn't mean you should forget about digital products or that they're only within the realms of those with massive email lists. But you do need to be prepared to be at it for longer before you replace your full-time income or make six figures.

If you have a much shorter timeline to work with, offering services will serve you better.

ASSUMPTION 2: COURSES ARE DIGITAL PRODUCT HOLY GRAILS

One of the biggest assumptions in the online space is that the only digital products you can create that are of value are premium courses.

You're nudged in this direction regardless of whether you have an audience or are just starting out in the online space.

Creating a course can certainly make you money, but there's *a lot* that goes into creating a course that sells.

Firstly, courses take a lot of time to create.

Especially if it's your first product, you may come out of it feeling frustrated and like you never ever want to create another course or digital product again. I've been there. Releasing my first course was and *still is* a painful memory.

Secondly, creating a catchall solution with a huge course is a dangerous proposition for a first-time creator because you're forcing your new audience into a "take it or leave it" situation when they're still getting acquainted with your brand.

There is a time and place for your signature or premium course. But your first product does not, and dare I say **should not**, be a signature course or premium product, especially if you're new to digital products, you're new to online business, and you're still growing your audience.

ASSUMPTION 3: IF NO ONE BOUGHT IT THE FIRST TIME, THE PRODUCT IS A FAILURE

I've seen people shelving perfectly good products because they were disappointed with sales or it didn't match up to this illusive idea of what they *think* a launch should be bringing in.

You will feel tempted to trash your digital product and create new ones, especially if it didn't get you the results you wanted.

But the last thing you should do is trash it.

What about the offer isn't working?

The lack of sales is always a symptom of some other problem.

Is the message of your product confusing? Are you not understanding your audience's pain points? Are your expectations even logical considering the size of your audience?

All products need a few iterations to test things out.

That's something that people don't really speak about.

ASSUMPTION 4: YOU'RE NOT "EXPERT ENOUGH" TO CREATE A DIGITAL PRODUCT

There's always going to be someone who knows more than you do on a topic. Someone who has more experience or who has coached more people.

But that someone does not have your unique perspective or background.

The online world is a noisy place.

It's easy to get comfortable and take others' views as your own.

But when you take the time to formulate your *own* response—your *own* take on something that's deemed as tried, tested, and true—you'll start to attract an audience who is genuinely interested in you, your brand, and your product.

Maybe you're saying, "I don't think this audience needs another offer with everything that's already out there!"

A crowded market is an opportunity when you know how to make your offer stand out. Offers differ in terms of price, the customers they serve, their promise, their style, or their mode of delivery.

If you map each competing offer against these elements, you'll realize that they all say something a little bit different. What you need to work on is finding the opportunity or empty "parking space" in the market for your digital product.

ASSUMPTION 5: THERE'S ONE MAGIC FORMULA

Everyone's business model is different and *should* be.

Your business model is a description of how your business makes money. It's how you deliver value to your customers.

My business model and why I do certain things look very different from someone else in the same niche as me. That's because it's modeled after my strengths and vision.

It's good to have a look at what others in the online space are doing. But just because a strategy, formula, or methodology worked for them, doesn't mean that it will make sense for you too.

So don't jump on that course or membership or [insert new and shiny thing] bandwagon just because it seems to be flashy and the next "in" thing.

The right questions to ask are

Why did it work for them?

Would it work for *you* considering your strengths, zone of genius, and what you want out of your business?

Can it be replicated?

Make your formula or methodology unique to *you*.

THE PLAN & HOW THIS BOOK IS ORGANIZED

This book is not the business equivalent of a "get-rich-quick" scheme.

This is not a book of stories and vague philosophies either. It's a practical guide with insights and strategies you can deploy to create a thriving digital product business.

If you've been winging it with the way you've been organizing and creating your digital products, the strategies outlined in this book will change how you approach digital products.

In **section I**, I'll walk you through how to stack your products and gradually escalate the experience that members of your audience have with you and your brand so that they keep coming back to buy more.

In **section II**, I'll walk you through the core areas of creating winning offers.

You'll see firsthand through case studies how the strategies taught in the book can be applied across three different niches—Pinterest marketing, fashion design, and visibility & PR.

In **section III,** you'll learn how to take everything you've learned and put together a digital product campaign. I'll also share with you the seven principles of becoming an extraordinary digital product creator.

If you've read my books *The One Hour Content Plan*[3] and *The Profitable Content System*,[4] you should be familiar with the system of categories and buckets I recommend using to organize and structure how you create content for your business. I'll briefly reference that organization system in this book as well because it's a part of your foundation and it all ties together.

A quick note: This book will not help you uncover your niche. It assumes that you have your niche figured out. If you haven't as yet, start with my book *The Blog Startup*.[5]

As with all my other books, *Selling the Intangible* aims to give you the tools you need to decide what will be best for you in your unique circumstance and niche. *You* decide how you want to utilize the strategies in this book.

If you dream of having a slew of digital products that your audience can add to their wish list and come back to buy from you repeatedly...

If you desperately desire a strategy and workflow for building a solid digital product-based business rather than constantly creating digital products, shelving them, and then going on to create new ones, only to have the cycle repeat itself...

If you want to tap into the gold- or diamond-dusted e-learning market, then this book will be right up your alley.

If you're ready, let's go!

You can download *The Intangible Playbook* and bonus resources at https://meera.tips/intangible. What's included in the bonus pack:
- Product Launch Sketch Template – The 10 blocks you need to be aware of before you even think about getting ready to put your product out there
- Digital Product Creator Tool Kit – Carefully curated tools and vendors to make executing your digital product effortless
- Proven steps to create, promote, and profit from digital products

SECTION I

UNCOVERING YOUR STRATEGY – PREPARING FOR EXPLOSIVE GROWTH

CHAPTER 1

OFFER & SUCCESS STACKING

My take on digital products revolves around two main points:

1. Always make the first sale easy—something low risk so that a potential buyer can dig into your paid content quickly, with the least resistance possible.

2. Structure your products such that your audience can come back and buy from you repeatedly.

You want to cultivate loyal customers, not buyers. When you focus on customers, you're focused on nurturing relationships and not just a single transaction. And it's important to note that the first sale is the hardest to make. It gets easier to sell to someone who has purchased from you before.

Someone new in your audience hasn't tasted your paid content as yet. They start by consuming your free content via your podcasts, YouTube videos, or blog posts. This free, ungated content may convince them to subscribe to your email list.

FREE CONTENT ------> **GATED CONTENT**

But how can you *decrease* the time taken from when someone becomes a subscriber to then going on to making their first purchase from you? How can you help *ease* that jump from subscriber to buyer to eventually a customer?

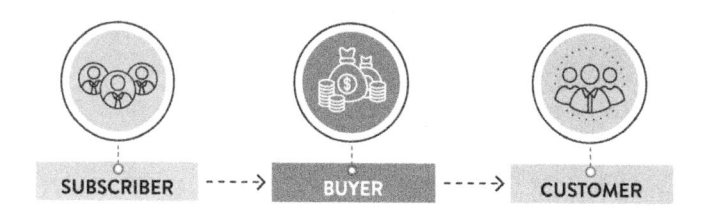

SUBSCRIBER ----> **BUYER** ----> **CUSTOMER**

Would that jump or transition be easier with a $39 or $2,000 product?

It's definitely easier with a lower-priced product!

Signature courses and memberships are a lot harder to sell than people will have you believe. When you are new to the online space or are just starting to build your audience, a course creates a huge paywall and makes it harder for your audience to say yes to your offer.

Why?

Because they're new to your brand. They're still learning to associate you with the topic of your offer. You're still building credibility and authority. As much as they may want to support you, a huge monstrous offer doesn't make it easy to say yes.

Likewise, a membership is a recurring fee. It's not a one-and-done transaction. People might be more hesitant to say yes to a recurring payment when they haven't gotten a taste of your paid content as yet.

We are so hardwired to think only about catchall courses, memberships, and premium products that we don't consider the potential of smaller products.

Remember that a signature or premium course or membership is but just one type of digital product. Here are examples of several other types of digital products:[6]

- **SPREADSHEETS**
- **AUDIO FILES**
- **PRINTABLES**
- **WORKSHOP/WEBINAR RECORDINGS**
- **STARTER 101 COURSES**
- **TEMPLATES**
- **MOCK-UPS**

Smaller or bite-sized digital products are easier to create and launch. And when you're still not used to creating digital products, you want something you can get out into the world fast, with the least resistance possible for you and your audience.

Is this a blanket statement for all businesses?

Of course not! And nothing is!

If you're selling consulting packages that cost thousands of dollars, having bite-sized products can be extremely jarring to your brand. But most of us don't sell packages or offers that cost thousands, making this a very viable option.

This is where a product ecosystem comes in.

A PRODUCT ECOSYSTEM OR OFFER STACK

A product ecosystem is a stack of offers that builds on one another and serves the different needs of your audience.

Your audience starts with a bite-sized product, often referred to as a tripwire or a loss leader. You can then go on to offer them a minicourse or signature course that dives deeper into the topic and their needs. For people in your audience who would love ongoing support from you, you can then offer them a membership.

Your audience progresses along their journey experiencing different outcomes and greater transformations with each product they consume. They interact with you at different stages of their journey and in different ways.

Have a look at the table below.

PRODUCT ECOSYSTEM – OFFER STACKING	
Product 1	Tiny Bite-Sized offer or tripwire (e-books, templates, minicourses, spreadsheets, mock-ups)
Product 2	Minicourse
Product 3	Membership
Product 4	Group Coaching Program
Product 5	VIP Day

Most of my clients and students who venture into digital products by creating a membership or course as their first product get stuck in creation mode. All that initial excitement quickly gets overtaken by overwhelm with *everything* they need to do and learn.

And naturally so!

Courses and memberships are hefty products spanning several videos and supporting material such as worksheets and workbooks. You're learning how to deal with the tech stack, how to create slides and film your videos, and how much to say and what to leave out.

But the struggles don't stop there!

If you do finally manage to crawl out of product creation mode, you may face a situation of *crickets* when you launch the offer. No one buys or very few people do because of reasons we'll explore later on in the book. But the entire fiasco makes you think that all that effort was for nothing.

I've been in that very same spot of overwhelm, defeat, and dread.

This is where a product ecosystem comes in.

It stacks your successes and builds your confidence as you grow your audience.

Smaller products give subscribers more reasons to buy from you rather than close all doors with a huge single sale like a $2,000 premium course. A client can stay with you for years and years because they are getting one solution after another that satisfies different needs and helps them achieve different outcomes. This is a piece of advice I wish I had when I started.

Let's take a look at different products at different tiers of solutions. I've also included revenue streams that are not digital products because it will give you an idea of where they are in the offer stack.

TIER 1

If you're still growing your audience and want to start monetizing your email list, create a front-end, low-risk offer such as a tripwire. Tripwires or bite-sized offers are Tier 1 digital products.

TIER 1

What's a tripwire?

It's a low-risk product you sell on your one-time offer page or thank-you page, usually as soon as a person signs up so that you can convert a new subscriber into a buyer quickly. Tripwires (often referred to as loss leaders) can be extremely profitable when done well. The main goal is not profit but to get that first sale.

LEAD MAGNET ----> ONE-TIME OFFER PAGE (TRIPWIRE) ----> EMAIL SEQUENCE

These products give your new subscriber a taste of your paid content, who you are, and how you can serve them. It piques their curiosity, helps to establish trust, and associates you and your brand with the topic of the offer.

TIERS 2 & 3

If you already have a buying audience and a low-risk offer, you can consider a starter course or a specialist or signature course.

A starter course is a foundational course or a 101. A signature course is a course that gives a complete transformation from A to Z. It has your signature framework, methodology, or formula of doing something. A specialist course is one main topic that you cover in detail. These are courses on topics that you are "known for" as the expert.[7]

STARTER 101 COURSES

TIER 2

SIGNATURE OR SPECIALIST COURSES

HYBRID (GROUP COACHING + PREMIUM COURSES)

SELF-PUBLISHING

TIER 3

TIER 4

If you already have a buying audience who resonate with your teachings or frameworks or methodologies and who identify you as a mentor, you can add a membership. A membership works when your audience see you as a regular, normal expense that is essential to their growth and success.

There are different membership models ranging from solely training-based memberships to those that are purely coaching and support-based. How you structure your membership, as I mentioned, is dependent on your goals, who your audience is, and how you want to serve your audience.

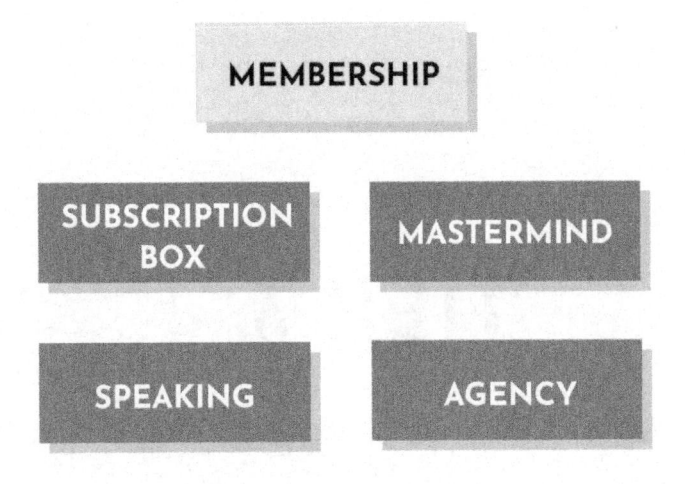

MEMBERSHIP

SUBSCRIPTION BOX

MASTERMIND

SPEAKING

AGENCY

TIER 4

Here's what each of the digital product tiers looks like.

REVENUE STREAMS

TIER 1	TIER 2	TIER 3	TIER 4
COACHING	STARTER 101 COURSES	SIGNATURE OR SPECIALIST COURSES	MEMBERSHIP
OFFERING A SERVICE		HYBRID (GROUP COACHING + PREMIUM COURSES)	MASTERMIND
TRIPWIRES / TINY DIGITAL PRODUCTS		SELF-PUBLISHING	SUBSCRIPTION BOX
AFFILIATE MARKETING			AGENCY
			SPEAKING

FAQ 1: Do I need to create products at every level?

No, you don't.

This very much depends on the revenue streams you want in your business and the audience you want to serve.

I have clients who are interested only in serving a 101 audience. Naturally, when you have helped this audience get past their startup or beginner phase, they will look to others to help them continue on in their journey to the intermediate and advanced stages.

While some see this as a *no-no* and a loss of opportunity, *you* decide who you want to serve. People will naturally outgrow how you can serve and help them, and this is a *good thing*! Why? Because...

1. You've helped them through that promised initial stages of transformation. Look at this as them graduating from your course or teachings.

2. If you speak to all audiences at different stages, you can end up speaking to no one.

The takeaway isn't that you should have an offer at every single tier or level. The takeaway is that catchall single solutions like huge courses or memberships are not the only options out there and to consider leading deeper transformation one product at a time.

FAQ 2: What if someone is an ardent fan and has bought all of your products? Do you still continue to create offers for them beyond your core and follow-up offers? What if there isn't anything more to offer?

You may likely encounter this situation somewhere down the road.

These are students and clients like I mentioned earlier who may have graduated or achieved that transformation that you have set out for your audience. There does come a time when someone may not need your business anymore. And that is what we all should aspire to—for clients and readers who have bought our products, taken action, experienced results, and who don't need us anymore. This doesn't have to be goodbye. You can invite them on as brand ambassadors into support groups for existing customers at the beginning of their journey. So it's OK to not create extra offers just to fill the pipeline.

FAQ 3: How soon is too soon to add a product?

I bought into the myth that "you need to give valuable content for six months before you've earned the right to monetize." But think about it...

If you have a solution to your audience's burning pain point, they're not going to count how many days or months you've been giving value before buying.

Yes, they may not know you as well...

Yes, you still need to build trust…

But if your free content is able to build just enough trust and you then go on to give them a low-risk, low-cost offer, then you've got a winner.

A tripwire is a great product to add especially if you've just started building your list.

But the type of tripwire you add matters. Create something too complicated and you lose the sale.

FAQ 4: How do I know if my first product is too big?

What's small or big? Look at the transformation of that product. That's an indicator of the size of your product.

The bigger the transformation, the higher the price point, and the bigger the product.

FAQ 5: How do I know what products to create in the ecosystem?

This depends on the specific pain points that you want to tackle or help your audience solve. We'll cover this in the next chapter.

CHAPTER 2

STAGE IDENTIFICATION

If you're familiar with my work and are on my email list, you may have seen this Stage Identification Sheet before. This is a framework that I, as well as several people in my audience, have followed. If you're looking for more clarity on when you should be attempting specific offers within the respective tiers, this sheet will serve as a guide.

It's not a hard-and-fast rule, and it's not meant to box you in. Its purpose is to serve as a guideline to help you make progress and avoid overwhelm and frustration.

STAGES

	STARTUP STAGE		GROWTH STAGE		SCALE STAGE	
	0	1	2	3	4	5
MILESTONE	Launch your biz with a solid foundation. Establish minimal viable plans.	Nurture & grow your list to 500-1,000 subscribers.	Earn your first $1K / Create and launch your first product or service.	Earn a full-time income. Expand revenue streams and sell products via evergreen funnels.	Expand revenue streams. Outsource noncore projects or tasks.	Automate selling of core or signature products. Put in place more systems. Incorporate paid ads into core strategy
HURDLE	Sleep learning curve. Lack of clarity. Shiny object syndrome.	Working at getting a consistent number of subscribers every day. Converting traffic to subscribers. Business costs when you're making nothing much/anything as yet.	Learning how to sell or launch. Feast or famine cycle.	Getting over resistance and blocks in investing. Learning how to sell effectively.		Balancing business expenses with need to grow your business further. Shifting into a CEO role. Knowing how to streamline and simplify for better results.
TEAM	Just You	Just You	Just You	You + Contract Help	You + Contract Help	You + Contract Help + Small Team
REVENUE	$0-$1K	$0-$1K	$1K-$3K	$3K-$5K	$5K-$10K	$10K-$30K
REVENUE STREAMS	Coaching Offering a service Affiliate marketing	Tripwire / tiny digital products	Signature or specialist courses hybrid (group coaching + premium courses)	Membership Subscription box	Mastermind Speaking agency	

CHAPTER 3
JOURNEY MAPPING

People at different stages in the customer journey have different questions and different pain points.

A pain point is a specific problem that prospective customers at that particular stage are experiencing. Understanding the problem you are solving for your customers is undoubtedly the biggest challenge you'll face when you're creating a digital product.

If you're familiar with my content and you've read my books *The One Hour Content Plan* and *The Profitable Content System*, you know that I'm a huge fan of the five states of awareness created by copywriting legend Eugene Schwartz.[8]

This states that a prospective buyer, reader, or subscriber starts by being problem unaware, then becomes problem aware, solution unaware, solution aware, and finally, most aware.

Have a look at the diagram below.

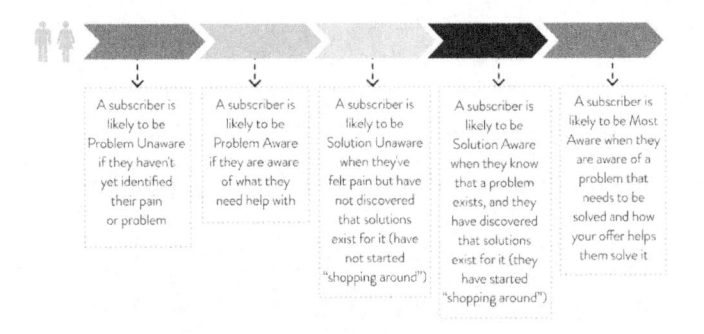

| A subscriber is likely to be Problem Unaware if they haven't yet identified their pain or problem | A subscriber is likely to be Problem Aware if they are aware of what they need help with | A subscriber is likely to be Solution Unaware when they've felt pain but have not discovered that solutions exist for it (have not started "shopping around") | A subscriber is likely to be Solution Aware when they know that a problem exists, and they have discovered that solutions exist for it (they have started "shopping around") | A subscriber is likely to be Most Aware when they are aware of a problem that needs to be solved and how your offer helps them solve it |

This is one way of thinking about buyer awareness.

Other concepts drop the reader (listener or viewer) into broader phases such as Awareness – Consideration – Decision, or into broad descriptions of Beginner – Intermediate – Advanced.

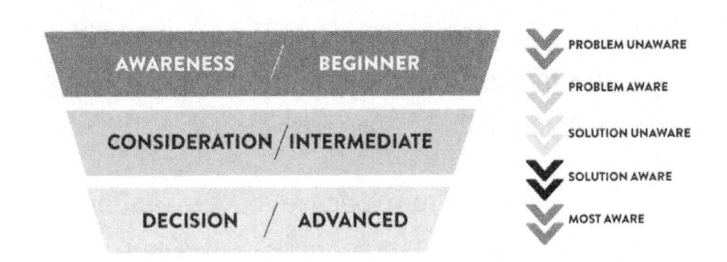

AWARENESS / BEGINNER

CONSIDERATION / INTERMEDIATE

DECISION / ADVANCED

PROBLEM UNAWARE
PROBLEM AWARE
SOLUTION UNAWARE
SOLUTION AWARE
MOST AWARE

SELLING THE INTANGIBLE

These frameworks can also be used as a guide to chart customer pain points. It's these pain points that will feed your product ecosystem and what digital product to create at each stage.

Here's a look at how pain points at different stages map onto the product ecosystem.

TIER 1 – These are top-level pain points. Imagine these as the pack of gum or chocolates they sell near the checkout counter at the grocery store. They never made it to your grocery list. You likely don't need them, but you have this impulse to purchase them either way! They offer temporary relief of the pain point but never really resolve the underlying problem. Some of your readers may have identified a symptom of a potential problem. They may not have identified the real problem but rather are looking for ways to soothe or get rid of their symptoms.

TIER 2 – They may be embarrassed by the questions they have due to their lack of knowledge about the topic in question. They're trying to read up on as much material as they can, and the topic is on their radar. Their pain points are centered around getting started and the "how."

How do I do [ONE ASPECT OF THE TOPIC]?

What tools should I use for [ONE ELEMENT OF THE TOPIC]?

How can I implement [TOPIC] to do [ONE ASPECT OF THE PROCESS]?

TIER 3 – They are hustling and trying out different strategies, but they are unhappy with the progress they are making or their results. *Why isn't this working for me? Why am I not getting these results? What can I do to get these results?* Their pain points are geared around specific solutions.

TIER 4 – They've tried to implement DIY solutions but have not had the progress or success they'd hoped they would have at this stage. Their pain points are centered around seeking connection, support, and access.

Here's an example of pain point progression of a client for my email marketing category.

Email marketing is so confusing. I know email marketing is important, but I don't know how to start.

I bit the bullet and signed up for an email service provider. Argh! But I don't know what to do next. How do I start growing my list?

I need email content ideas. I don't know what to send or what to even say in my welcome email series.

How do I write emails that sell? I have products that I want to sell on auto via an evergreen email sequence, but how do I do that effectively?

Depending on your niche and audience, there may be overlapping pain points between different levels. But how do you know what people want or what they will pay to get rid of their pain point?

The best (and worst) advice I've ever heard?

Ask your audience.

Do your audience really know what they want?

No, they don't.

This is why I don't recommend running surveys to your entire list to ask them what they want.

One of Henry Ford's famous quotes goes as follows: *If I had asked people what they wanted, they would have said faster horses.*

Instead of forcing your audience to discuss solutions that they don't yet appreciate or fully recognize, get them to discuss problems or symptoms they have.

If you're thinking of running a survey, send it out to your customers or fans. These are people who have bought from you and most likely will buy again. Remember, it's easier to get a repeat purchase than it is to get a brand-new sale.

But what if you can't ask your audience what they want, or you don't have access to an audience because you're just starting out?

How can you test the viability of a product then?

How do you know if this is something people will pay for?

There are lots of signs that can give you an indication of whether you've hit product gold.

Here are some places that are teeming with insights you can get about your ideal buyer.

- Amazon book categories (look for categories in your topic and the top 1–20 books)

- Udemy (look for the number of registrations and ratings)

- Other people with similar products in your niche

- BuzzSumo (articles trending for your keywords)

- Pinterest

You also want to look out for the following:

- What questions do people keep asking?

- What questions are always coming up in your niche?

These questions show you that there's a need—that people are looking for ways to solve this problem.

So have your ears to the ground and try to tap into what your audience is seeking out.[9]

To keep the content in this book updated, I've listed a few tools I use to do audience research in the bonus kit instead. You can access it here > https://meera.tips/intangible.

While it's important to consider (a) what your audience will pay to get rid of their problem, and (b) the presence of similar products in the marketplace, you don't want to neglect another important component—**YOU**.

- What you are excited to teach
- Your skill set
- How you are two steps ahead of your ideal buyer

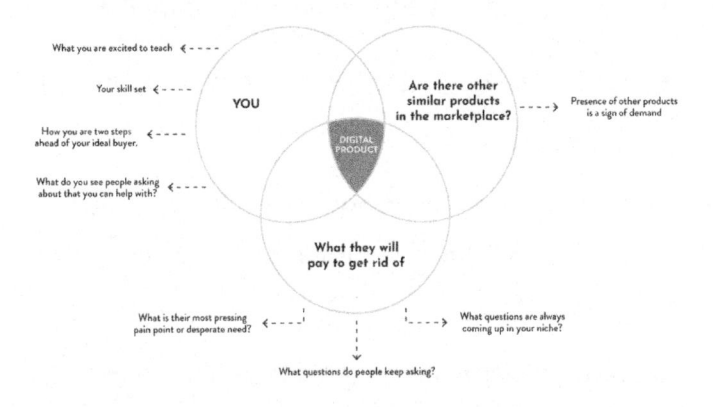

What you are excited to teach

Your skill set

YOU

Are there other similar products in the marketplace?

Presence of other products is a sign of demand

How you are two steps ahead of your ideal buyer.

What do you see people asking about that you can help with?

DIGITAL PRODUCT

What they will pay to get rid of

What is their most pressing pain point or desperate need?

What questions are always coming up in your niche?

What questions do people keep asking?

You want to work on a product that excites you.

You want to be committed to a product idea. Because, as you will find out further into the book, just because an offer doesn't sell as well the first or second time around doesn't mean the idea is moot.

You need to see a product through the launch process a couple of times even if you are tempted to scratch it and start over. It takes a few iterations to know how to hit the right pain points and how to position your offer well.

This takes a certain degree of commitment to the outcome of your offer and how it can help your audience. We'll talk about how to craft the right offer in the next chapter.

Now, let's apply the product ecosystem to our case studies.

For each case study, I've given several options depending on the different pain points that can be tackled. In some case studies, I've also shown how you might integrate a done-for-you option with digital products.

I'd like to reiterate that there are no rules. Do what's best for your zone of genius, who you want to serve, and the vision you have for your business. You can also choose to target and serve certain pain points and not others. You can choose to have offers at some levels and not others.

MEERA KOTHAND

CASE STUDY – PINTEREST SPECIALIST

Cath teaches entrepreneurs how to get started with Pinterest.

AUDIENCE PAIN POINTS SHE CAN TACKLE:

- o How do I create click-worthy images when I have no time?
- o How do I design click-worthy images without any design background?
- o How can I increase traffic from Pinterest?
- o How can I increase traffic from Pinterest and convert that traffic to sales?

OPTION 1	She can start with a Tier 2 Pinterest 101 course that shows her audience how to get started with the platform—show them how to set up their boards and profile and walk them through the basics of Pinterest descriptions and keywords. She can then go on to offer a Tier 3 signature course that showcases her Pinterest framework or secret source to getting traffic and turning that traffic into profit. LEVEL 1 ----> LEVEL 2 PINTEREST 101 / PINTEREST TRAILBLAZER TO TURN TRAFFIC TO PROFIT

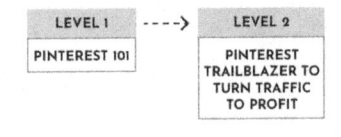

SELLING THE INTANGIBLE

OPTION 2	Alternatively, she can offer a Tier 1 tripwire to people struggling to make Pinterest images. She can then offer her 101 and signature courses followed by a membership that offers click-worthy Pinterest image templates every single month. 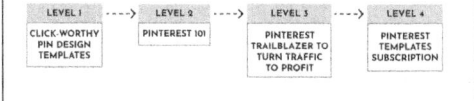 LEVEL 1 ----> LEVEL 2 ----> LEVEL 3 ----> LEVEL 4 CLICK-WORTHY PIN DESIGN TEMPLATES / PINTEREST 101 / PINTEREST TRAILBLAZER TO TURN TRAFFIC TO PROFIT / PINTEREST TEMPLATES SUBSCRIPTION
OPTION 3	She could also offer a Tier 3 specialist course just for people who want to be Pinterest virtual assistants (a subset of her audience) and help them get the skills needed to manage their clients' accounts. 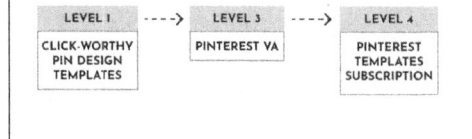 LEVEL 1 ----> LEVEL 3 ----> LEVEL 4 CLICK-WORTHY PIN DESIGN TEMPLATES / PINTEREST VA / PINTEREST TEMPLATES SUBSCRIPTION

CASE STUDY – FASHION DESIGN

Lena serves people who want to become fashion designers but don't have any formal education. Most of them are working a 9–5 with the dream of starting a fashion boutique in the future.

AUDIENCE PAIN POINTS SHE CAN TACKLE:

- How do I do create easy sketches that can be turned into clothes?
- How do I design clothes for myself?
- How do I design profitable clothes people want to buy?
- How do I start a fashion boutique?

OPTION 1	She can start with a Tier 1 Fashion Sketch Template Pack, which can be offered as a tripwire. This can teach her audience how to start sketching designs that people will love. This is an extremely searched-for topic and will grab her audience's attention. She can then offer a Tier 2 101 course on how to get started with designing their first or next fashion collection. She can then offer a Tier 3 signature course that provides an A–Z transformation and takes someone from idea to launching their own boutique.

LEVEL 1		LEVEL 2		LEVEL 3
FASHION SKETCHES TEMPLATES	-->	DESIGNING A FASHION COLLECTION	-->	START YOUR OWN BOUTIQUE

SELLING THE INTANGIBLE

OPTION 2

Alternatively, she can offer a Tier 1 Fashion Sketch Template tripwire to people struggling to make sketches. She can choose to offer a Tier 2 101 course to help people start on their journey to becoming a fashion designer.

She can then offer a specialist course on how to design their first or next fashion collection. Finally, she can offer a Tier 4 membership that gives resources and monthly trainings that take someone from the idea phase of starting a fashion boutique to launching it to keeping it profitable from month to month.

Note: If you notice, the same product "START YOUR OWN BOUTIQUE" is positioned as a membership in Option 2 but was positioned as a signature course in the earlier option.

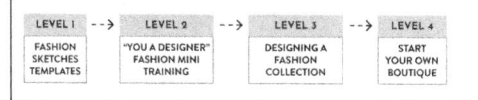

LEVEL 1	-->	LEVEL 2	-->	LEVEL 3	-->	LEVEL 4
FASHION SKETCHES TEMPLATES		"YOU A DESIGNER" FASHION MINI TRAINING		DESIGNING A FASHION COLLECTION		START YOUR OWN BOUTIQUE

CASE STUDY – VISIBILITY & PR

Joan helps female entrepreneurs grow their businesses through strategic public relations.

AUDIENCE PAIN POINTS SHE CAN TACKLE:

- How to pitch hosts and journalists so that you get noticed
- How to find the best places to pitch that will give the best ROI
- How to implement PR without much time

OPTION 1

She can offer PR Pitch Templates for TV, radio, online magazines & podcasts complete with spreadsheets to track pitches and a short video training on the dos and don'ts of getting started with PR. She can then go on to offer an in-depth DIY course for small business owners who want to start getting noticed through strategic PR. This will be a starter solution and will take someone from nothing to crafting a strategic PR plan for their business even if they don't have a lot of time, are starting from scratch, or have failed at PR before. She can then provide a monthly subscription of curated targeted journalist and podcast host requests that fit students' areas of expertise.

TIER 1	---->	TIER 2	---->	TIER 4
PR PITCH TEMPLATES		STRATEGIC PR		CURATED PR

OPTION 2 | Alternatively, she can start by offering her Tier 1 PR Pitch Templates. She can then choose to offer a hybrid signature course for small business owners who want to start getting noticed through strategic PR. This hybrid solution will give students a one-to-one coaching option and the opportunity to have their PR plans reviewed and personally vetted.

She can offer a premium done-for-you service where a tailor-made PR plan is crafted based on a strategy call and reviewing the goals of the business owner.

TIER 1	---->	TIER 2	---->	TIER 2
PR PITCH TEMPLATES		STRATEGIC PR		PR INTENSIVE

ACTION

Can you chart your own offer stack or product ecosystem? Or if you have existing digital products, how do they stack with each other?

If you've read my books *The One Hour Content Plan* and *The Profitable Content System*, you know that I recommend using a system of categories and buckets to organize and structure how you create content for your business. Each content category can have its own product ecosystem or offer stack.

SECTION II

THE ESSENTIAL DIGITAL PRODUCT KIT – ORGANIZING & BUILDING YOUR PRODUCT FOR SUCCESS

Have you put your heart and soul into creating a digital product only to have it launch to crickets?

You thought it would work and then it just didn't.

I've been there.

I've sold only three spots of a $97 program.

Sure, it was still three sales, but I was devastated.

I thought I had the sales page right. I thought I was being clear. I thought I was giving people what they asked for.

But I stuck with the offer.

I worked through the messaging. The marketing. The sales page.

Now?

It's an offer that brings me a full-time income each month.

Looking back, I see all the mistakes. The pieces that were not done in the right order. The focus on the completely wrong components.

Haphazard wouldn't even *begin* to explain how I worked on that digital product.

Creating a digital product has so many moving pieces. How do you put everything together in a way that doesn't leave you overwhelmed *and* gets your audience excited to buy from you?

This is exactly what we're going to delve into in the next few chapters.

CHAPTER 4

WHY PEOPLE DON'T BUY YOUR STUFF

Most of the time when you want to create a digital product, you jump right into thinking about the format of the product.

How many videos it is going to have...

What you'll be charging...

The tools you need, and so on.

All of these are logistics that should come later on.

Instead of thinking about your product and jumping the gun in the process, begin thinking about your offer or solution.

You can have a great product but a terrible offer.

Offer versus product. These are two different entities.

Your **product** in simple terms is the nuts and bolts of what they get. These are the features.

PRODUCT
Number of videos
Number of worksheets
Number of chapters
Facebook support group
Slack support channel

The **offer** or **solution** is how you package your product.

OFFER
Outcome/Promise
– How can you frame your product so that it's most attractive to your ideal buyer?
Note: You don't sell your offer to everybody. You only need to spend your time and resources attracting your ideal customer. If you had a "poster boy or girl" for your brand, this would be them.

> Your offer vs. other similar offers in the market
> – What can you tap into that the rest haven't? What's the real reason someone will be motivated to spend money on *your* offer instead of other people's offers?

Look at your offer through your ideal customer's eyes.

- Who would benefit the most from what you offer?

- What promise or product outcome will be the most attractive to *your* ideal customer?

- What result can they expect if they buy and implement what you're selling?

- If you're adding bonuses, what will push them to say "YES" to your offer?

- Do they immediately understand how your offer makes their lives easier?

- How are you going to package your product and position it relative to others in your niche or market?

- What's that unique *X* that a customer can get from your product that they can't get elsewhere?

- What's the real reason someone will be motivated to spend money on *your* offer and not other people's offers?

The answers to these questions will form your offer or your package.

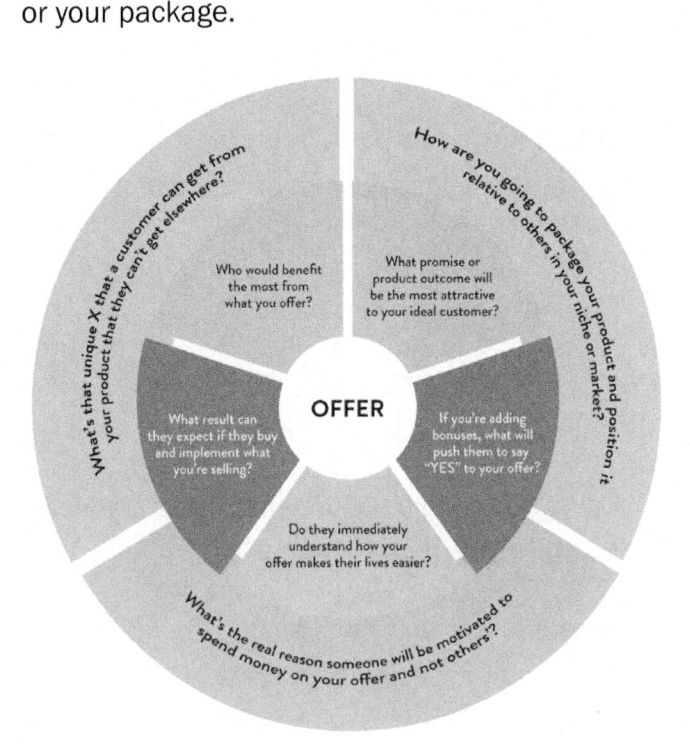

What's that unique X that a customer can get from your product that they can't get elsewhere?

How are you going to package your product and position it relative to others in your niche or market?

What's the real reason someone will be motivated to spend money on your offer and not others?

Who would benefit the most from what you offer?

What promise or product outcome will be the most attractive to your ideal customer?

What result can they expect if they buy and implement what you're selling?

OFFER

If you're adding bonuses, what will push them to say "YES" to your offer?

Do they immediately understand how your offer makes their lives easier?

SELLING THE INTANGIBLE

These are elements that you tend to ignore till *after* you create your product.

Packaging your offer should be as, if not more, important than creating your product. This isn't something that you can whip up *after* you create your product.

You can only do this at the **start** of the product creation process. Because if you do, you'll know exactly how much needs to go into your product and what you need to do to convince your ideal customer.

People don't spend money on the information in a digital product because it looks pretty or helpful. They spend it because they have a goal, and they believe this information will help them achieve that goal.

Having a promise, outcome, or goal gives your digital product some tangibility. It's easier for a reader to grasp what your digital product hopes to deliver. It makes selling the intangible easier. No pun intended.

Product = What you do

Why anyone cares = The outcomes you deliver

Harvard marketing professor Theodore Levitt put it brilliantly: "People do not buy drill bits, they buy holes."

People don't buy products. They buy outcomes.

So how do you decide how to package your offer?

STEP 1 – DETERMINE WHERE IN YOUR PRODUCT ECOSYSTEM THIS PRODUCT GOING TO BE

What exactly are the characteristics of this product? Is this a tripwire, a starter 101, or a specialist or signature course?

Identifying where in the product ecosystem this product will take its place will help you define its package further.

STEP 2 – CONSIDER THE COMPETITION AND THEIR OFFERS

Most people cringe at the word competition or competitors.

If you're uncomfortable with this, think of these as players or people or influencers operating in the same space as you.

The presence of other products in the market is a good sign—a sign that there's demand for that product in the market.

But that doesn't give you a right to cough up what everyone else is offering.

To give your product the best possible chance of success, you want to create a well-defined package that's different from what's out there. To do this, you first need to identify who your competitors are.

How you do this could differ based on how far along you are in business. Some of you may already have offers. Some of you might just be starting out and growing an audience.

Let's tackle both of these situations.

YOU HAVE AN EXISTING OFFER

1. Who does your audience compare your offers or content against?

How different is your offer from Person A's Offer X?

I was considering your offer or Influencer B's offer.

Have you received comments like these?

These comments are gold because they highlight who your audience would approach if you didn't exist. You may not see these people as competitors. You may even think they engage in a conversation that is completely different from the conversation you're having.

But what you think doesn't matter.

You want to be the obvious choice for your audience, and to do this, you need to identify the options they are choosing from.

2. If you didn't exist, where would your audience go?

Who would *you* refer your audience to if your product didn't exist?

YOU DON'T HAVE AN EXISTING OFFER

1. Who are the others with similar offers in the same category?

SELLING THE INTANGIBLE

Start by defining your offer in its simplest form.

Heard of the duck test?[10]

"If it looks like a duck, swims like a duck, and quacks like a duck, then it probably is a duck."

Is this a course on **email marketing**?

Is this an e-book on **stitching**?

Is this a workshop on **dating**?

That category is the conversation you are a part of.

Who are the others with similar offers in the same category?

What other products deliver on the benefits or value of products in the category of your offer? These are your direct competitors.

2. Who are the others with *adjacent* offers in the same category?

You don't just consider those offering a digital product, but also those who offer services or coaching in the same category.

Often, we tend to only look at people who have similar business models. For instance, when you only consider people who are course creators, you may neglect the voices who are in the same niche but in different business models such as coaching or done-for-you services. These are your indirect competitors.

When you look at adjacent alternatives or substitutes, you'll then be able to identify all relevant players in the marketplace.

STEP 3 – DO AN AUDIT

Based on who you have identified, do a content audit of your competitors' products.

- What promises are they making?
- What bonuses are they giving?
- What headlines are they using?
- Who do you think is their ideal customer?
- What are the core messages being shared?

STEP 4 – PICK A FIGHT

- **Central idea being shared about each of these offers**

- What's your gripe with the central idea?

- Here are some central ideas I always pick a fight with:

    - Everyone should create a course/membership

    - Teaching email sequences by saying that you only need seven emails[11]

- **Methodology/How-to**

- What don't you like about their methodology or way of teaching?

- "How-to" or methods I always pick a fight with have to do with choosing a lead magnet based on the pain points of your audience. I propose an alternative method of choosing a lead magnet.[12]

- **Why should a buyer choose you over every other available option?**

    Are you serving a specialized subset of an existing audience?

    Do you have a unique framework/methodology?

There are so many ways you can be different.

Having the answers to these questions will help you know how to package your offer and present it to your audience.

The earlier you think about it, the more successful your product will be.

You may not always nail your offer the first time. That doesn't necessarily mean that people don't want your product or don't like it. It takes a few iterations to know how to package your offer the right way.

SELLING THE INTANGIBLE

- What if you feel like you don't have any competitors?

This isn't really a good thing. It means
    a. It's likely that there isn't a demand for products or services in this market.
    b. Others have failed to effectively monetize this niche.
    c. You're not looking in the right place. The keywords or terms you use to define your niche aren't those that your target audience is using or what other businesses use.

ACTION

If you already have a digital product, how well defined is your offer? Is there a clear point of difference between your offer and what's out there? Have you "picked a fight" using at least one of the three points mentioned in Step 4?

CHAPTER 5

FROM SKELETON TO FLESH

Spend at least 30% of your product creation time on outlining the product.

When you don't have a solid outline, you create more or less content than you actually need.

Worse, you create content that doesn't align with the desired outcome or promise of your offer.

What transformation do you intend to achieve for this digital product? Have a look at some examples below.

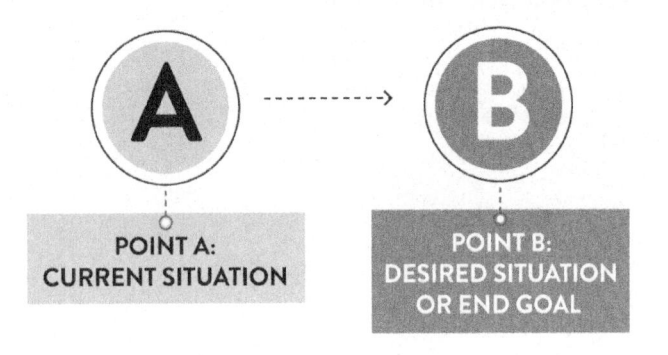

POINT A: CURRENT SITUATION ----→ **POINT B:** DESIRED SITUATION OR END GOAL

SELLING THE INTANGIBLE

MY PIN IMAGES LOOK UGLY  --> **I CREATE BEAUTIFUL PIN IMAGES IN HALF THE TIME WITH THESE TEMPLATES**

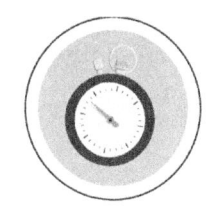

I DON'T HAVE TIME TO GO TO THE GYM TO WORK OUT  --> **I JUST NEED 20 MINUTES A DAY AND NO EQUIPMENT TO FEEL GREAT AFTER MY WORKOUT**

I CAN'T COMMAND HIGHER RATES BECAUSE I'M NOT A SPECIALIST PINTEREST VA AND DON'T KNOW HOW TO NAVIGATE PINTEREST --> **I'M GETTING BOOKED OUT BECAUSE OF MY SPECIALIST PINTEREST SKILL SET**

Depending on the type of digital product you're creating, you would

1. List out the steps required to take someone from Point A to Point B

2. List out the mini-milestones or goals someone requires to go from Point A to Point B

For instance, 101 or starter type products likely have steps or lessons to reach a specific transformation.

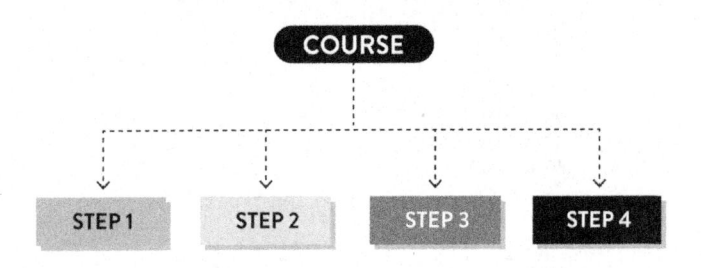

```
                    COURSE
        ┌─────────────┼─────────────┐
        ↓         ↓         ↓         ↓
     STEP 1    STEP 2    STEP 3    STEP 4
```

Specialist or signature offers, likely those in Tier 3, are modular in nature. Each module has a specific goal that nudges your audience toward the transformation. Asking yourself the question "What do you need to know to achieve that specific goal or milestone?" breaks down the module further into individual lessons.

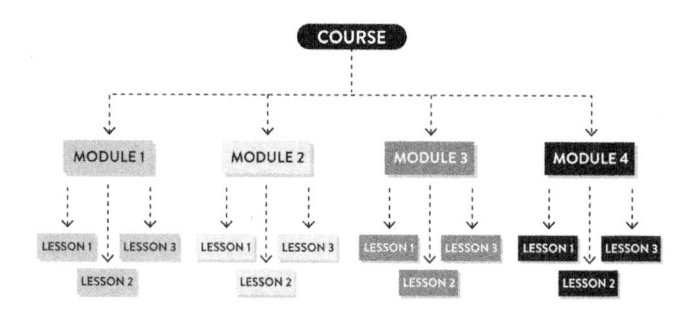

```
                    COURSE
         ┌────────────┼────────────┐
         ↓            ↓            ↓            ↓
      MODULE 1    MODULE 2     MODULE 3     MODULE 4
      ↓  ↓  ↓     ↓  ↓  ↓      ↓  ↓  ↓      ↓  ↓  ↓
   LESSON1 LESSON3  LESSON1 LESSON3  LESSON1 LESSON3  LESSON1 LESSON3
     LESSON 2        LESSON 2        LESSON 2         LESSON 2
```

Asking yourself the question "What will make it easy to implement?" will break it down further into supporting materials such as worksheets, swipe files, or templates.

This tells you exactly what you need to cover so that the goal is accomplished.

Anything else that doesn't directly relate to the transformation or goal can be used for your bonus content. When you do it in this way, you provide just what is necessary.

Because one of the mistakes that creators make is to include too much in their product. And I've made that mistake as well.

ACTION

If you already have a digital product, think about the structure explained above. Have you included more or less content than is necessary? If you're thinking of creating a new digital product, can you use the model above to flesh out your content?

CHAPTER 6

OUTSTANDING SALES PAGES

Heard of the saying "Eat that frog"?

Get your sales page written and out of the way as soon as your product outline is done.

Since I started doing this, I always have a clear direction as to what I'll include in my products.

It also takes a big stress point away because you can use content from your sales page in your prelaunch and sales phases, which we'll talk about in the next few chapters.

This way you know you will always be consistent with your messaging.

A sales page has several sections.

Long form or short form, every single section on the sales page has to convince your ideal customers that your offer is for them.

Have you heard people bragging about five- and six-figure sales pages?

Can a sales page account for the entire success of your launch? No, it can't.

A sales page is important. But a sales page on its own cannot deliver radical success for your digital product.

It's just one component in the entire process.

The supporting content that leads to your sales page, how you establish credibility, the follow-up process and the email content you send after you've sent someone to a sales page *all* matter as well.

When you have a failed launch, it's not just your sales page that has to be analyzed but other elements of the process too.

How do you write your sales pages and blog posts faster?

The answer: prework and structure!

A sales page is a hefty piece of copy.

I use what I call the Copy Triage or Grid Mapping System that highlights nine key elements from start to end.

Take a look at any of my sales pages and you'll see these nine elements reflected.

WHO

Who will benefit the most from this offer? Are they

1. Problem Aware

2. Solution Aware

3. Problem Unaware

HOOK

- Encapsulate the primary benefit, why they should care about solving the problem, and what they are looking for

PAIN POINTS

- What problems are you solving?

- What symptoms do your target audience experience in their own words?

CHANGE

- List out the change or transformation you're promising.

- What does the "rainbow" on the other side look like for them in this situation?

PRODUCT INVENTORY

- List out the bullet points of what you're offering.

The lifeblood of your sales page is the bullet point.

Surprised?

Have a look at your favorite sales pages. The bullet points tease and build anticipation.

They give you just a tiny peek into the offer and get you excited to buy. Your bullet points need to do that.

MYTH

- List out commonly held myths holding people back from making this change or from taking the actions you need them to take.

OBJECTIONS

List out all the objections people have when it comes to the offer. These could be objections related to money, their own limiting beliefs, the time they have to work on the offer, or even the offer itself.

FAQ

- What questions do people have before they say yes to this offer?

ACTION

Is your digital product sales page missing any of these elements? Take note of which elements you can incorporate or improve on.

- Your product should have its own branding.

This doesn't mean it has to be drastically different from your own brand. Pick cues from your existing brand.

This could be the look and feel, an accent color, or a font. It can have its own branding but still be complementary to your current brand.

But a word of caution.

As with anything branding, it can be a huge time suck.

It can be a reason to procrastinate.

NAME

Always choose clear over clever.

It's a lot easier to come up with a name after you've defined the value proposition or promise of your product.

Your name should capture the essence of what your product will do for your readers…if it can give them a glimpse of the after.

Clever and creative names leave a potential buyer confused and do more harm than good.

LOOK & FEEL

You don't need to have an ultra-fancy product logo, images, or slide templates. You don't need to get these done by a designer either.

These are bells and whistles that can be added later and revamped as you grow.

I'm all for investing in tools, but tools shouldn't become a reason to delay the launch of your product. We all have to start somewhere, and as long as your product collaterals and materials are neat and organized, you're good to go!

CHAPTER 7

PERFECT PRICING

In every sale there's a gap.

Your customer ———> Their future state

YOUR CUSTOMER **THEIR FUTURE STATE**

The larger the gap, the higher the price point.

How you price your digital products depends on

1. The value of the outcome you are helping your customers achieve

2. How much the outcome is *worth* to your customer

In the majority of cases, price isn't what stops a customer from buying; it's the **perceived value of your offer**.

The perceived value increases the more your solution fixes their problem. People buy when they're in pain and in need of a solution to a problem. Every digital product has to be an answer to a problem.

However, it's up to you to help potential customers understand this. It's up to you to demonstrate this value.

This does not mean listing out what they get—the features. It involves focusing on outcomes and results. So always highlight the benefits and not the features.

We'll talk about this in the next chapter as well.

Another way to determine your price is by plotting out a price spectrum.

1. Plot out the brands in your niche and where along the spectrum they fall. List out their prices.

2. Circle the brands you want to be associated with.

3. Where do you fall on the spectrum? Or where along the spectrum do you want your brand to be placed? Plot it out.

Here are some common scenarios when it comes to pricing:

1) *How dare you make a profit from your work?*

I've had subscribers and clients write to me in tears because of nasty comments from people in their audience chiding them for making a profit from their products or coaching just because they're in the wellness, faith, or budgeting niches.

Never apologize for selling your work or wanting to make a living especially when you've followed through on the steps above. People need to know you're in business too.

2. *Your price is too high.*

Have you communicated the value of your product? How does your value compare with your competitors?

Are you unknowingly attracting the wrong audience?

Think about where most of these leads or subscribers are coming in from. Are they joining your list from a particular content upgrade or lead magnet?

Is that lead magnet attracting the right audience who will be keen on going on to buy your products and services? Or is there an audience-offer mismatch?

While we can't delve into email marketing in detail here, I talk more about relevance in my book *300 Email Marketing Tips.*[13] The higher the degree of relevance between every single component in your marketing system, the higher your engagement, sales, and overall subscriber satisfaction will be.

But no matter how well priced your products are or how much value you give, there are some people in your audience who will have an issue with the price point no matter what it is.

Leave these people out of the equation. If their claims are completely invalid, do yourself and them a favor and click unsubscribe (for them).

For everyone else, some resistance is good. If no one has a problem with your price, it's a signal to raise it.

Have this in mind the next time you send a sales email and are afraid people will unsubscribe.

A key point you need to remember is that value and price point must be aligned.

If you're selling a massive five-module course for $39, the value doesn't align with the price point. This sends a mixed message about the true value of your product. *If it's so cheap, it's probably not good.*

This is why we determine where in the product ecosystem a product is as a first step. It helps to set your expectations right.

ACTION

Does the value of your existing digital product align with your price point?

CHAPTER 8

LAUNCHING YOUR PRODUCT IN TODAY'S ONLINE SPACE

Have you ever been in a store and needed help with picking something out?

Or maybe you had a question about a product you were thinking about purchasing?

In situations like these, a *can I help you with something* from a salesperson is more than a welcome interruption.

The best buying experiences you've had are probably with salespeople who made you feel happy and comfortable with your purchase.

There's no pressure or hard selling involved.

That's how it should be when you're selling your products to your audience. People overcomplicate selling. Selling, like anything, is best when it's simplified.

An old business saying goes "People love to buy. But they don't like to be sold to."

As an online business owner, you're increasingly engaging with a far more aware and mature audience.

There used to be a time when a three-part video series was exciting. But now your audience's defenses go up when they hear you have a three-part video series. They know they're going to be sold to.

You can't knock on the door once and expect a flood of sales immediately. You can't show up today with a "cart-open" email and get your people to throw themselves at your sales page. Persistent nurturing and knocks on the door win in today's online space. The internet has tipped the scales of information and power from sellers to buyers.

So how can you convince someone to buy rather than force the solution on them?

This is where education comes into play.

Education is the new selling. As Zig Ziglar said, "You will get all you want in life if you help enough other people get what they want."

The job of a successful seller is to guide buyers and provide value at every single step.

Selling or launching a product, when done right, provides immense value to everyone. It creates a win-win for you and your audience.

Everyone comes out of it educated and aware of your topic even if they don't end up buying. You get massive awareness for your offer. The ones who don't buy are a step closer to buying the next time around or the one after that.

People don't mind the interruption. They only mind if the interruption doesn't make any sense to what they think they're there for.

When in doubt, ask yourself the following question: if you remove your sales pitch, does your content still add value?

This is why you need to prime your subscribers for the sale.

When you have a strategy in place, you'll have more people who welcome your interruption than those who don't. Before we dive into how you can prime your audience, let's get the definitions out of the way.

WHAT A LAUNCH IS NOT

Many clients I speak to think that all they need to do to launch their digital product is to stick it at the end of an email sequence for people to find.

Yes, people may discover your digital product as they go through your email sequence, but that's not the first thing you should do.

There's a difference between live launching your offer and having it sell on evergreen.

When you live launch your offer, you have fixed open- and close-cart dates. There is a specific period of time within which someone can buy your offer. People don't see this offer again until your next launch.

But when you sell an offer on evergreen, it is <u>always available for sale and is not tied to launches or open and close carts.</u>

It ensures you have a steady source of income rather than the income highs and lows associated with a business model built solely on live launches. Launches bring in a huge portion of revenue and then clam shut the moment you close cart.

Have a launch one month, and you'll bring in loads of revenue.

Don't have one the next month, and your revenue source has dried up.

Going evergreen on your offer is an excellent way to keep the sales momentum going postlaunch. This is useful because people prefer to buy in different ways. Some need the hype and energy of a live launch to buy. They thrive on events held around a live launch and want to interact directly with the digital product creator before making their decision.

Others want to buy an offer on demand when they *need* it and are perfectly comfortable buying via an evergreen email sequence.

Both a live launch and an evergreen email sequence have a place in your marketing calendar.

For instance, I have my courses running on evergreen in the background, but I also do occasional live launches as well.

We'll discuss going evergreen in the next chapter, but for now, let's take a look at the different elements in a launch and the types of launches.

ELEMENTS OF A LAUNCH

Element 1: Prelaunch Phase

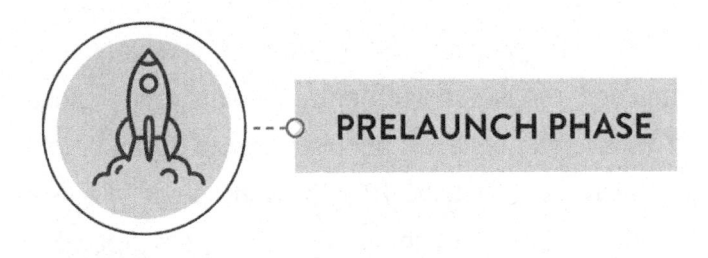

PRELAUNCH PHASE

The most underrated element in a launch is a prelaunch.

I still see entrepreneurs showing up on or just before cart-open date and announcing that their offer is for sale. If your cart opens tomorrow, you should have a prelaunch phase at least 3–4 weeks in advance. Because if you don't, then you're not engaging your audience.

You're not preparing them to buy from you.

You're not addressing questions or objections they may have, prior to the sale.

This is one of the biggest reasons launches flop.

Most prelaunch campaigns aren't really prelaunch campaigns at all. Most have a message *"I have a huge surprise in store for you"* or *"I have something I'm really excited to share"* under the guise of a prelaunch.

Now, you can of course be excited. But your prelaunch phase has to answer three of the questions below:

Does your audience even know that this is something that needs to be solved?

A prelaunch shouldn't just get your audience excited by the impending launch of your offer; it should prime them as well. You do that by creating content around the topic of your offer. People can't appreciate a solution to a problem that they don't know needs fixing.

Your first step is to help your audience clearly understand their current pain so they can see and feel how much these problems are costing them, holding them back, and preventing them from experiencing what they want.

Make them aware of the topic. Get their attention.

Talk about mistakes they may be making around the topic. You're building anticipation before you even mention your offer as a solution to this problem they've now become aware of. You're getting them interested in the topic.

Note: Always use their own words to describe their pain and to describe their ideal vision.

How can they solve these pain points or problems?

What content can you provide that points them in the direction of solving the mistakes/pain points you pointed out earlier?

Do they know how things could change by solving that pain point?

Get them to see the light at the other end of the tunnel.

What are the possibilities?

What's in it for them?

How could this solution potentially change their lives?

Paint a picture of how their lives could be. What content can you provide that increases their desire for wanting your solution?

This is when you soft sell your offer and mention that your offer is about to be released.

Element 2: Sales Phase

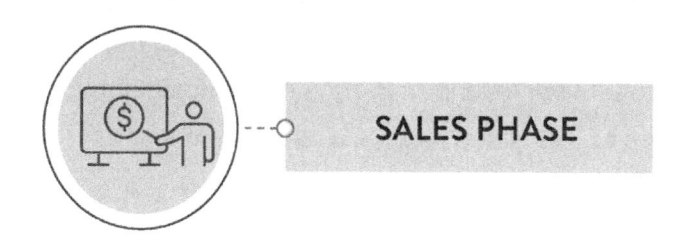

SALES PHASE

Do they know what solutions are out there and how yours is different?

Have you removed objections they have against your product?

Have you answered questions they have about your offer?

You want to brainstorm and jot down as many ideas as you can for these questions based on your offer. Then start to outline content pieces (emails/blog posts/videos/podcasts) that will feed your prelaunch and sales phases.

This is exactly what I walk you through in my book *The Profitable Content System.* If you want to know the exact types of content pieces that will prime and nudge your audience, have a look at that book.

If your audience is not convinced they need your offer, and if they have objections that your offer won't work for them, then sending those subscribers to your sales page is a conversion killer even if it was written by a star copywriter.

You want to send subscribers who are primed to buy your offer…

Subscribers who are convinced they have a problem that needs solving...

Subscribers who have had their objections countered...

As good as your sales page is, it can't work miracles, especially if people are not primed or convinced.

Element 3: Urgency and/or Scarcity

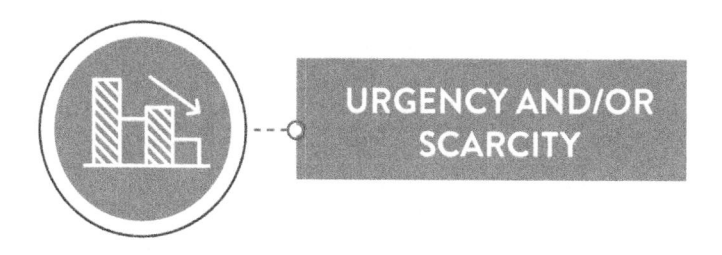

URGENCY AND/OR SCARCITY

Let's be honest.

You and I don't take action unless we have a deadline. So if you think imposing a deadline is manipulative, it's time to shift your mindset on that. Urgency is a good sales tool.

There are three ways in which you can introduce urgency when you sell your digital products.

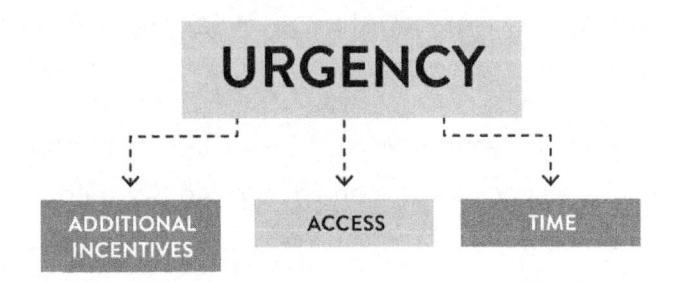

URGENCY
- ADDITIONAL INCENTIVES
- ACCESS
- TIME

- Additional incentives
  - Various fast-action bonuses
  - Surprise bonuses
  - Limited quantities
- Access
  - Access to creator's time
  - Lifetime access with free upgrades
- Time
  - Limited time

TYPES OF LAUNCHES

There are several types of launches.

You can do simple under-the-radar email-only launches. These are launches that involve using purely email to communicate with your audience, and these emails signify the open- and close-cart dates for your digital product. You still need scarcity and urgency. You still need a fixed open- and close-cart date and time. But email does the heavy lifting.

UNDER-THE-RADAR LAUNCHES

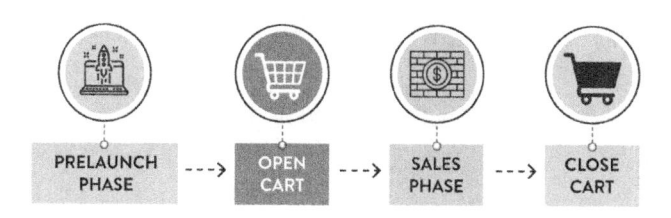

PRELAUNCH PHASE ---> OPEN CART ---> SALES PHASE ---> CLOSE CART

Some launches involve using a "vehicle" like a webinar, challenge, workshop, or masterclass that helps to open cart to your offer.

LAUNCHING WITH A VEHICLE SUCH AS A WEBINAR

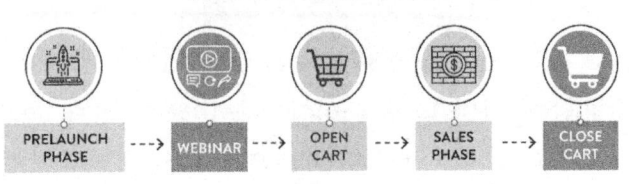

PRELAUNCH PHASE ---> WEBINAR ---> OPEN CART ---> SALES PHASE ---> CLOSE CART

LAUNCH VEHICLE
- WEBINAR
- LIVE STREAM SERIES
- WORKSHOP SERIES
- CHALLENGE
- MASTERCLASS

Regardless of whether you utilize an under-the-radar launch or a launch vehicle, all launches need the three elements we discussed above:

- Prelaunch Phase

- Sales Phase

- Urgency & Scarcity

Most people find launches tiring.

I agree. Launches can be high-intensity periods and cause loads of overwhelm.

As much as you may hate the emotional stress that comes with launching and want nothing to do with that and as eager as you are to sell your offer automatically to make some passive income, I can't stress enough that you need to live launch your offer first.

You want to have at least a 1–2% conversion rate comfortably before switching it to evergreen.

Why?

Because live launches help to validate your offer.

What exactly is validation? Validation is proof that you know your offer converts, that the webinar topic you've chosen taps into your audience's pain points, and that your emails are able to nudge your audience and convert to sales.

Can't you validate these through an evergreen sequence or evergreen webinar?

You can. But it's a lot easier to do it during a live launch.

Once you know you have a set of elements that work, you won't be going in blind with your evergreen funnel, which we'll talk about in the next chapter.

FAQ 6: If video scares you, does it mean you won't be able to launch any product successfully?

No, you're not doomed just because you don't use video. Video scared me for the longest of times too. But under-the-radar (or email-only) launches work equally as well!

CHAPTER 9

SECRETS TO SCALING YOUR OFFER

How do you get consistent eyeballs on your offers?

Maybe you launched it to your email list and got ten sales that first week. You emailed them again the week after and the numbers dwindled.

You're getting anxious because you can't seem to hold your audience's interest in your offer anymore. Sales drop to single digits and then ultimately go to zero. You feel like the snake oil salesperson repeating your offer to your email list week after week after week.

Is there an alternative?

Yes, there is!

You let evergreen funnels do the job for you.

A funnel is the journey a subscriber takes toward the end goal you've set. It's a strategic, well-thought-out plan that inches the subscriber toward the products and services you offer. You can have an automated webinar funnel that pitches your course. You can also have an evergreen funnel that pitches your e-book or a five-part video series funnel that pitches your membership site.

Here's an example of how an evergreen funnel could look.

BLOG POST (WITH CONTENT UPGRADE) ---> THANK-YOU PAGE ---> EMAIL SEQUENCE OF TEN EMAILS WITH AN OFFER TO BUY PRODUCT A

So even if a brand-new subscriber who's potentially interested in your offer only joins your email list after your live launch, he/she doesn't have to wait another four months till you have another launch to see that offer.

You can still get eyeballs on your offer via your evergreen funnels.

When you have evergreen funnels—especially for your bigger offers—your income doesn't swing drastically from one month to the next.

Now, revenue fluctuations are normal in any business.

But what you **DON'T** want are huge swings that are often represented by extreme peaks and troughs.

This usually happens when you have a launch or promotion one month and don't the next.

What you want is a system that will allow you to have a predictable source of income rather than be at the mercy of a launch.

This is so that you can

- Keep getting sales from month to month.

- Get incoming payments from people who purchase via your payment plans.

- Cater to people who are early adopters and readily buy via your evergreen funnels rather than make them wait for your next live launch.

"Evergreening" your offer is the best way to keep the sales momentum going postlaunch.

But when should you *wait* to go evergreen?

- When you haven't validated an offer as yet. Always live launch it first as I mentioned in the earlier chapter.

- When it doesn't deliver the same results or impact as it does live.

- You can't go evergreen on an offer that's positioned as a high-level mastermind, coaching program, or live workshop. Your audience will not buy into the offer because the hands-on live nature of the offer is lost in an evergreen funnel.

Here are the aspects behind an evergreen funnel strategy:

1. A hypertargeted lead magnet that keeps the freebie hoarders away and attracts only people

who resonate with the pain point of your offer. This does not necessarily have to be your webinar or masterclass.

2. A sequence of emails that
3. a. doesn't give away the farm,
4. b. is salesy or self-serving, and
5. c. doesn't have you afraid to ask for the sale.
6. An element of urgency
7. Always have urgency, even in your evergreen funnels. This could be disappearing bonuses, price increases, close-cart time urgency, or even a mixture of two or more of these elements.
8. A tool that helps you set an evergreen timer.
9. Video recording (for webinar funnels).

The average conversion rate is 1–2 %, and your evergreen funnels can have these very same conversion rates. This means that you can expect to sell 1–2 copies for every 100–120 people who go through your funnel.

The more people you get into you funnel, the more you can expect to sell, especially if you have a funnel that is validated.

FAQ 7: Do you need webinars for all your funnels?

Does a simple $17 or $39 e-book need to have a webinar in your funnel?

Not necessarily.

Webinar funnels do work well, but you don't always need them. Email funnels are absolutely viable as a standalone.

So it's not about doing something because everyone is doing it. It's about whether it serves the goal of your funnel.

And you can have various combinations of funnels with varied traffic sources and different opt-ins as well as different end goals.

You can have one funnel pitching a small $39 e-book and another pitching a $397 product.

But the simplest funnels are all you need to start bringing in revenue.

If you do intend to create an evergreen webinar, don't create one that leaves your audience cringing, squirming, and gagging. You don't need to (you shouldn't) fake the live element because it isn't live. Your audience is OK with it not being live.

The real secret to creating an evergreen funnel that generates sales doesn't rest on expensive technology or faking elements of a live launch.

CHAPTER 10

TOOLS

How exactly do you go about selling your digital products?

For many people, this is the first thing they consider. But I've intentionally placed this chapter toward the end of the book because this isn't the most important aspect.

Figuring out your strategy should be the most important consideration before you even think about tools. Because what happens—and I've seen this happen far too many times—is that you can end up going down a rabbit hole of considering tool after tool after tool and losing sight of the bigger picture.

To avoid confusion (if tools get discontinued or drop in standard), I will avoid mentioning specific names of tools in this chapter. To know the exact rolodex of tools I use, you can check out my bonus tool kit here > https://meera.tips/intangible.

I always suggest looking at three things before picking any tool:

1. Price point

2. Whether it can grow with your business without you needing to upgrade or switch to another one midway

3. How easy it is to use considering your comfort level with tech

Here are the main tools you need in your tool kit to start selling digital products:

1. Any landing page tool that has templates or the ability to create sales pages

Note: Many email service providers come with landing page functionalities, but these templates are often only for lead generation, and they can't be customized for sales pages unless you're familiar with coding.

2. A shopping cart to collect payments

3. A platform to host your content securely

4. A countdown timer to create real urgency/scarcity

5. An email service provider to automate your email follow-up and sales sequences

The easy "all-in-one" option

There are all-in-one tools that will host your content, provide a payment gateway, collect payments, and also host sales pages.

Depending on the plan you choose, most all-in-one platforms charge a monthly fee and may also take a percentage of each sale.

Other options provide only a checkout or shopping cart to collect payments, but you still need to figure out how to host your content. For simple downloads, Dropbox, Google Drive, or any secure cloud storage option is also feasible. But if you plan on offering videos and multiple pieces of content within your product, it's best hosted on a content or course platform for your students' ease of use.

FAQ 8: Should you sell on an external marketplace like Amazon, Udemy, or Coursera vs. on your own site?

This very much depends on the goals you have for that offer. Many of these marketplaces have their own rules. For your offer to be favorable in the eyes of these marketplaces, you need to follow their system of writing descriptions or keywords or structuring your offer. Selling on your own site gives you more flexibility but may not get you as much reach as external platforms.

Pricing is an issue as well. A $2.99 book is common on Amazon and isn't seen as low quality. But the same e-book priced at $2.99 on your site might be seen as low quality. Likewise, certain topics don't do as well on certain platforms and might do better on your site.

I could have sold my books *The One Hour Content Plan* or *The Profitable Content System* as courses but chose to sell them as e-books on Amazon instead after weighing the pros and cons as well as my intent for both offers. So consider your intent for your offer as well as the pros and cons of selling on an external marketplace vs. on your own site.

SECTION III

BUILDING YOUR DIGITAL PRODUCT BUSINESS – HOW TO 10× PRODUCTIVITY & PROFITS

Let's take a step back and review everything we've covered.

You discovered how you can use the product ecosystem to plan out the digital products that you can create. You also learned how pain points your audience have at each stage of the customer journey can fuel your digital product brainstorming.

You then went through various core components that you need to consider *while* creating your digital product that contribute to the success of your offer. One of those components is understanding that packaging and marketing your product should be as important, if not more important, than creating your product.

All of these elements form your meat. These ensure that you have an organized system of creating digital products so that they're not haphazardly put together.

Think of this final section as the gravy that supports the meat dish and gives it character.

In this final section, I'll walk you through how it comes together in a digital product campaign. Everything we have discussed up to this point in the book are elements that will feed that product campaign.

I'll also introduce you to seven potent principles I hold on dearly to. These principles will help you create an audience that will keep coming back for more.

CHAPTER 11

YOUR FIRST OR NEXT DIGITAL PRODUCT CAMPAIGN

Say you decide to create a digital product today.

What happens first? What happens next?

Let's walk through the twelve steps that will take you from idea to launch. Pay close attention to Step 6 so you set your expectations right!

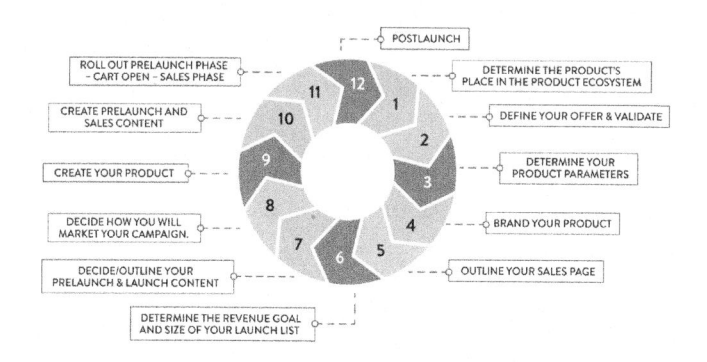

- 12 POSTLAUNCH
- 1 DETERMINE THE PRODUCT'S PLACE IN THE PRODUCT ECOSYSTEM
- 2 DEFINE YOUR OFFER & VALIDATE
- 3 DETERMINE YOUR PRODUCT PARAMETERS
- 4 BRAND YOUR PRODUCT
- 5 OUTLINE YOUR SALES PAGE
- 6 DETERMINE THE REVENUE GOAL AND SIZE OF YOUR LAUNCH LIST
- 7 DECIDE/OUTLINE YOUR PRELAUNCH & LAUNCH CONTENT
- 8 DECIDE HOW YOU WILL MARKET YOUR CAMPAIGN.
- 9 CREATE YOUR PRODUCT
- 10 CREATE PRELAUNCH AND SALES CONTENT
- 11 ROLL OUT PRELAUNCH PHASE – CART OPEN – SALES PHASE

STEP 1 — DETERMINE THE PRODUCT'S PLACE IN THE PRODUCT ECOSYSTEM

STEP 2 — DEFINE YOUR OFFER & VALIDATE

Think about what they will walk away with after consuming your product or service?

What goals or benefits will they achieve or attain?

How is this offer different from other offers out there?

Look at the market.

A market consists of a group of products with similar characteristics. Scan the market for the existence of other similar offers.

STEP 3 — DETERMINE YOUR PRODUCT PARAMETERS

Outline your product based on the goals and benefits defined in Step 2.

What does your content need to cover so that the buyer gets the promised outcome/result?

What format will you be offering this in?

What bonuses and supplementary content will you be providing?

STEP 4 — BRAND YOUR PRODUCT

STEP 5 — OUTLINE YOUR SALES PAGE

Long form or short form, every single section on the sales page has to convince the ideal buyer that your offer is for them.

STEP 6 — DETERMINE THE REVENUE GOAL AND SIZE OF YOUR LAUNCH LIST

Often I would hear clients and students say that their launch was a flop because they only sold X number of pieces but were intending to sell Y.

Before you determine that your launch is a flop, you need to determine the possibility of those numbers.

I came across a quote in a book: As motivated as the cyclist is to reach 100 km/h, a cycle isn't designed to reach those numbers. Motivation is but one tiny part of the puzzle.

You can be very motivated, but if your campaign isn't designed to hit those numbers, no amount of motivation or drive or planning will get you there.

You need to reverse engineer your revenue goal to see if it's possible in the first place.

How do you determine a revenue goal for a campaign?

You don't just pluck this number from thin air. You can do this in the following ways:

1. Based on past data

If you know from past experience that you can make $5K on this campaign, that gives you a good gauge of what to expect.

2. Based on the size of your email list and estimated conversation rate

With an email list of one thousand at a 2% conversion rate, you can expect to make twenty sales.

3. Based on your income goals for that campaign

I need Y number of people in my launch list so that at an estimated 2% conversion rate, I will meet my sales target of ____.

A launch list or interest list is a group of people you have identified as being interested in your offer. This could be a specific segment of your email list. Or if you're going to have a launch vehicle for your campaign, this will be the number of people who sign up for your launch vehicle.

Take into consideration the following:

- Revenue goal
- Program price
- Units to sell
- Conversion rate (1%–2%)
- Number of leads needed (your launch list or interest list)

Revenue goal: $5,000

Program price: $200

Units to sell: 25

Conversion rate: 2%

25/0.02 = 1,250 leads or subscribers

You need at least 1,250 people on your launch list to comfortably hit your revenue goal.

If you want to include ads into the picture, here's how it'll work out:

Average cost per lead estimated at $2-$6

Organic leads: 500

Ad leads: 750

Budget: $1,500-$4,500

Profit: $500-$3,500

New leads: 750

STEP 7 — DECIDE/OUTLINE YOUR PRELAUNCH & LAUNCH CONTENT

What launch vehicles (if any) will drive your campaign?

- Webinars

- Challenges
- Workshops
- Video series
- Email-only campaign

What type of prelaunch content will "speak" to your ideal customer? Remember to address the following questions to support your offer's prelaunch phase:

- Does your audience even know that this is a problem that needs to be solved?
- How can they solve these pain points or problems?
- Do they know how things could change by solving that pain point?

Remember to address the following questions to support your sales phase content (after cart open):

- Do they know what solutions are out there and how yours is different?

- Have you removed objections they have against your product?

- Have you answered questions they have about your offer?

What urgency factors will you use?

- Additional incentives

- Access

- Time

STEP 8 — DECIDE HOW YOU WILL MARKET YOUR CAMPAIGN

How you market your campaign will be based on the type of launch you planned for.

Are you doing an under-the-radar email-only launch or will you be using launch vehicles?

You need to get people on your email list to run a successful campaign. How are you going to attract and capture those people?

You can take a four-prong approach to marketing any campaign:

- Your existing email list
- Organic marketing on traffic platforms
- Paid ads
- Influencer sharing

If you already have an email list, you could get people to sign up for your launch vehicle or market your offer to them. At the same time, you also want to attract new subscribers. This is where you want to promote your campaign or the specific launch vehicle on the traffic platforms you use such as Pinterest, LinkedIn, or YouTube.

STEP 9 — CREATE YOUR PRODUCT

STEP 10 — CREATE PRELAUNCH AND SALES CONTENT

STEP 11 — EXECUTE YOUR PRELAUNCH PHASE, CART OPEN & SALES PHASE

STEP 12 — POSTLAUNCH

How much revenue did your campaign earn?

Did you meet your sales target?

How did it compare to previous campaigns you ran?

If you didn't meet your revenue target, try to pinpoint why this was so.

Is it because you didn't have enough people going through your campaign to meet the goal?

Or is it because your sales page didn't convert, although you had a healthy click-through rate?

Determine which content pieces and emails performed the best. Identify which content pieces didn't hit the mark as well.

The following will give you clues:

- High impressions, but low conversions
- High open rate, but low click-through rate

I recently had a subscriber write in to say that her launch was a flop because she had only sold three of her $500 course.

Was it really a failure?

What do the numbers *actually* say?

Has she reached the right conclusion?

Sure, on the surface three is a small number. But how many people actually clicked through to her sales page?

I bet if she looked at the right numbers, she would see that she probably exceeded the typical 1-2% conversion rate we can expect from launches.

You don't want to be blindsided by emotion. You could focus your time and energy on how you can bring in more revenue rather than fixing something that wasn't broken in the first place.

So always go back to *what do the numbers say?*

FAQ 9: Something converted well before but doesn't now. What do you do?

Consider the following factors:

- Is it the timing?

Is the timing right for your audience?

Have you launched your product during summer or elections or any important holiday?

You don't have to avoid holidays or events when launching your product, but keep in mind that your audience may not be able to focus on your launch because of external factors.

- Has the conversation in the space shifted?

What resonated with your audience before may not do so now. If the conversation in the space has shifted to other focus areas within your niche, your content has to reflect that shift as well. It's very important to know that your message is resonating with your market. You want to make sure you and your audience are on the same wavelength and that your message is striking a chord.

- Have a guarantee or return policy for your product

There are people who will buy a product just to ask for a refund.

I've had a person ask for a refund two minutes after their order came through citing the product lacked everything that it actually already includes.

Having a guarantee shows people that you're confident about your work. It takes away that pressure of having all their hesitations solved before getting the program. It provides a safety net for them to fall back on especially if they are new to your brand.

Yes, there are a couple of people who do take advantage of the system. They may call in your charge as fraudulently entered.

Is it painful? Sure, it is.

But realize that this is the reality. It's not just you. Everyone in the online space goes through this.

Be prepared for it and don't let it ruin your day.

Does it have to be a 30-, 60-, or 90-day guarantee? No, it doesn't.

You know your program best. If a shorter guarantee period makes sense for your program because of the way it's structured, go ahead and do that.

CHAPTER 12

SYSTEMS TO RUN IT LIKE A WELL-OILED MACHINE

Systems are processes that you can set up once and then automate.

In this chapter, we'll take a look at a few different systems you can set up including your payment processor, offer hosting platform, and email service provider.

EMAIL AUTOMATIONS

There are several features within email service providers that allow you to set up different systems with varying benefits for your digital product business.

But a quick warning that this very much depends on the capabilities of your email service provider.

I've also used terms such as *tag, link trigger*, and *segment*, but these same features could go by a different term within your email service provider. Let's take a look at some situations where automation and systems can play a key role in boosting your sales.

ONBOARDING SEQUENCE/POSTPURCHASE EMAIL

This is a touch point that many people miss out on. You don't want to leave your new customers in limbo after they purchase.

What should people do first or next? Even with a solid system in place people can get overwhelmed and confused. It's your job to help them get unstuck. You want them to continue to feel confident in the choice they made.

If it's a higher-priced offer that they've just purchased, you can also consider scheduling a postsale or onboarding sequence.

The goal of a postsale sequence is to guide your buyer through using your product as well as negate buyer's remorse.

Some ideas for postsale sequences:

- A guided sequence through each of the modules or chapters, even if the product is not dripped out
- A solid welcome email that highlights the transformation they can expect to make in the next few days or weeks
- An email that allays their fears about falling behind or losing access, etc.
- An email with any surprise bonuses for those who finish or an unexpected bonus

A SUBSCRIBER CHECKED OUT YOUR SALES PAGE

Identify anyone who's clicked on your sales page link in your email with a tag called "Prospect." You can then send them tailored email content where you call out that you're aware they've seen the sales page and invite them to ask further questions about your offer.

Clicked Sales Page > Tag subscriber as "Prospect" > Subscribe to Cart Abandon Email Sequence

YOUR SUBSCRIBER JUST PURCHASED YOUR PRODUCT

When someone purchases your product, tag them as "Purchased Product X" and then send out an automatic welcome email sequence for that product or connect them to a new email sequence that handholds them through your course or product.

You can also exclude subscribers who have this tag from receiving any further sales emails about this product.

Purchase product > Tag subscriber as "Purchased Product X" > Subscribe to Thank you for purchasing email

Purchase product > Tag subscriber as "Purchased Product X" > Subscribe to Onboarding Sequence

A SUBSCRIBER HAS FINISHED GOING THROUGH YOUR COURSE OR PRODUCT

Set up an automated email that goes out a set period of time (e.g., thirty days) after someone purchases your product or completes your welcome sequence and asks them for a testimonial. This way you'll get your much-needed social proof and do it on auto. You will wake up each morning to testimonials in your inbox rather than have to actively look for them or remember to get in touch with subscribers, customers, or clients.

Purchase product > Tag subscriber as "Purchased Product X" > Subscribe to Onboarding Sequence > Completed Onboarding Sequence > Subscribe to Testimonial Sequence

ACTION

What systems can you implement? If you already have digital products, what ideas come to mind that you can implement?

CHAPTER 13

PRINCIPLES OF EXTRAORDINARY DIGITAL PRODUCT CREATORS

Having digital products in various formats and being the primary component of my business model, there are some simple but profound truths that I rely on to this day.

Call these my *mantra* if you will.

PRINCIPLE #1: CHOOSE STRATEGY OVER TACTICS

Tactics can change. But strategy rarely does.

Strategy is the plan—the map or the route to your destination.

Without this plan or map, you won't be able to figure out the tools or tactics you need to bring along for your journey.

If you find yourself spending too much time mulling over what course platform to choose or what design to use for your worksheets, you're focusing your energy in the wrong place.

You cannot use tactics unless you have a well-thought-out strategy. Strategy should guide everything you do as a creator.

PRINCIPLE #2: DON'T GET SWAYED BY BIG NUMBERS

What's the actual profit from a six- or seven-figure launch?

The numbers tell a one-sided story.

Even if you do hit six or seven figures, are you keeping the money that you're generating? What many entrepreneurs don't share is that they could be paying the bulk of their revenue to copywriters, Facebook ads, and other tools.

If you make $100K for a launch with overheads of 85% from hiring copyrighters and ad managers or running the ads yourself, you take home $15K.

If you make $20K for a launch with overheads of 25%, you take home $15K—the very same amount.

In both cases, the take-home profit is the same, but the effort is different.

Always weigh the effort vs. the impact vs. the profit.

Is it worth it?

PRINCIPLE #3: COMPARE APPLES TO APPLES

It's easy to look at someone else's numbers and be blown away.

But look at the numbers that matter and then compare them with yours. Yes, you're operating on a smaller scale, but are you getting the same (or better) results than they are?

Look at the right numbers...

Look at their expenditure (ad spend, consultants, designers) for that launch. Look at their conversion rate for the size of their launch list. Look at the defaults and refunds. Note: You might not have access to your competitor's data unless they share income/expenditure/review reports and updates.

These are the numbers that give the correct picture.

How do your launches fare when compared to these?

Compare apples to apples. You can't compare a 50,000 launch list to a 10,000 one. It's about the ratios and percentages. Those don't lie.

So when you're demotivated thinking about your numbers, pause and dig deep. Your reality might actually be better than you thought it was.

PRINCIPLE #4: WORK ON BEING TOP OF MIND—ALWAYS

I'll be ready the next time. Please send me the launch emails when it's out.

Keep selling this to me.

I'm not ready now. But I will be one day.

These are some of the emails I've received from subscribers when I've launched a digital product. And you honor that. You keep enriching them with content. You sell to them because they gave you permission to do so. I'm not talking about icky, sleazy hard selling.

But how do you be top of mind?

Through email and content.

Quit thinking of email as a magic bullet.

I'm a huge fan of email marketing. Yet, I don't think it's a magic bullet. You can't show up one fine day, write an email, and expect to rake in sales. Maybe this was possible years ago, but not now. Likewise, you can't depend on magic launch formulas to mysteriously bring in thousands of dollars in sales. They only work if you've been working at being top of mind.

But what if people don't buy during a launch?

A launch, when done right, enriches your audience and educates and empowers them even if they don't buy from you. Even if your audience doesn't buy from you right away, you're still serving them with content that builds your authority and gets them to associate you as someone they can trust with the topic of your offer. And who knows? They may become a customer and brand advocate down the road!

You continue to show that you are there, even if they're not ready to buy yet.

According to Brian Carroll, author of *Lead Generation for the Complex Sale*,[14] almost 95% of your audience or subscribers are not ready to buy. But 70% of them will *eventually* buy from you or your competitors.

This is where content comes into play.

You score with your content marketing if that 70% think of you and come to you when they're ready. It's beyond the scope of this book to cover content in detail, but if you want to put in place a content marketing strategy that aligns with your business, have a look at *The Profitable Content System*.

PRINCIPLE #5: NEVER BE AFRAID TO MENTION YOUR OFFER EARLY

If you're running a five-day campaign for your digital product launch, your launch list should hear about the offer at least 2-3 days before you open cart to the offer.

You want to get them familiar with your offer. You want to build desire for your offer before the cart even opens.

And that can't happen if you don't talk about and keep it top secret before cart-open date. Anticipation and curiosity are good. But waiting too late to introduce your offer can do more damage than good.

Everything I've walked you through in this book will help you build a strong foundation to market your product. If marketing does its job, the selling or launch process won't feel salesy because you won't have to convince your audience of the pain point, the problem, your method, or your authority.

PRINCIPLE #6: DO THINGS THAT DON'T SCALE

You're always told to outsource things that don't scale.

But you need to remember that you build your brand one person and one interaction at a time. In the early days, everything moves terribly slowly, and it may feel like you're not making progress at all. Subscribers trickle in slowly. You'll get one subscriber a day, or maybe two subscribers. It doesn't seem like much, but every single one of them signed up to hear more from you.

With the right mentality, you can nurture them to become customers. So build relationships. Focus on the long term—on the things that won't impact your bottom line immediately (e.g., strategy, systems). Focus even on the things that don't scale and that people tell you to outsource like engaging with your audience.

These will set you up for **BIG** success in the coming months (and years).

Focusing on long-term, "slow and boring" growth is the fastest way to scale.

PRINCIPLE #7: SOLVE THE RIGHT PROBLEM

I've worked with lots of clients, and the three main problems I see are with

- Business model
- Audience
- Sales

Let's tackle your business model.

Your business model is how you make money. This usually involves you spending time to create and deliver programs. You need to expend effort to research and package up your offers, and you need to spend money on systems or tools that will allow you to be in business. These include your course hosting platforms or payment processors, scheduling software, etc.

Problems occur when you choose your business model based on what you could/should/would do. This is often based on seeing what others are doing or on trends or on what's "in." When your business model is not in alignment with your strengths and your stage of growth, you will expend more time, energy, and effort than it should take. It can become almost torturous working on your business because three steps forward will take you two steps back.

Let's tackle your audience.

When it comes to audience, you expend time and effort in finding and converting readers into subscribers. You have to build trust and nurture your audience. You have to build content-expert association (so that you avoid having a sales problem!).

Problems here are two-fold. Either (a) you don't have systems in place to nurture your audience, or (b) the brand and audience you're trying to attract are completely different.

Let's tackle sales.

You have to master the sales process. You have to put in time and energy to figure out which launch vehicles and messaging your audience responds to best.

The problem with sales is that it might not even be a sales problem in the first place. You can throw more resources into solving what you think is a sales problem, only to find out it is in reality an audience problem!

So don't throw your resources at solving the wrong problems. You can't jump through a stage in business. Yes, you can do it faster, but you can't ignore the foundation.

CONCLUSION

You now have more than a bare-bones framework to put in place a digital product strategy for your business.

Remember that is all about the long game.

You aren't running a sprint; you are focused on the marathon! You are focused on improving and celebrating small wins **DAILY**.

You don't reach your goal in one jump; it takes every little step to help you get there.

Whether it's ads, tools, or live events, I've seen a lot of my subscribers bite off more than they can chew when they are creating and launching their digital products. They add too many variables into the picture when they haven't validated any one of them as yet.

They think more work would, and should, equate to more cash flow and higher revenue streams. This leads to more confusion and overwhelm.

Many of them don't end up launching their product at all. I'm a huge fan of under-the-radar launches because they allow you to test a bare-bones framework. Once that works, then add one element after another into the equation.

With every stage that I've crossed, I've found you do need a different set of skills, but that's the easy part. **The mindset is what will trip you hard.**

Just because you fail once, doesn't mean your product sucks. It doesn't mean your content's bad either.

Putting a digital product out there is a process. It takes several iterations to get it right (as does your mindset).

This is NORMAL.

And if you've spent thousands on coaching and classes and still feel like you're getting nowhere,

I can assure you that it has nothing to do with you not having the necessary marketing or business skills.

It has *everything* to do with your mindset.

If you're desperate for the sale, that desperation sneaks into your copy.

If you think people shouldn't be paying $X for a digital product, that doubt is going to hinder you from having someone pay YOU that $X.

If you think you're greedy to charge $Y for your course, you're likely self-sabotaging yourself with that very sale.

If you don't think you could ever sell digital products or sell online, you're probably not going to be able to do so.

Achieving growth and success isn't a linear upwards curve. It's gradual.

On several days you may feel like you're not making any progress. Like you're not moving the needle at all.

Everything you're doing is just "building on the foundation."

But you may not realize that your daily actions build, grow, and stack.

There is a breaking point where the compound interest you've been accumulating via your incremental, consistent actions starts to pay off.

I don't know where you are in your online business journey.

Maybe you're just getting started. Or perhaps you're in the beginning stages and thinking about your first digital product. Or maybe you already have digital products, but they haven't done much for your business...

Trust in the process. Do the work, and watch the profound effect it has on your business.

That's the secret to how businesses "magically" take off.

I want you to feel like you can do this, and I hope the next few months hold a digital product launch for you.

Before you go, remember to download your bonuses at https://meera.tips/intangible.

Good luck and thank you for sharing your work with the world!

THANK YOU FOR READING

I hope you enjoyed reading this book.

I really appreciate your feedback, and I love hearing what you have to say.

Could you leave me a review on Amazon letting me know what you thought of the book?

Thank you so much! If you want to get in touch, come find me here at my slice of the internet: https://www.meerakothand.com.

Meera

ABOUT THE AUTHOR

Meera is an email marketing strategist and 3× Amazon best-selling author of the books *The One Hour Content Plan, But I'm Not an Expert! & Your First 100*. She is also the publisher of MeeraKothand.Com, an award-winning site listed as one of the 100 Best Sites for Solopreneurs in 2017, 2018, and 2020 and the popular CREATE Planners. Using her unique Profitable Email System™ and ADDICTED™ Business Framework, she makes powerful marketing strategies simple and relatable so that small business owners can build a tribe that's addicted to their zone of genius.

Other Books on Amazon

RESOURCES

1. Bobby Chernev, "27 Astonishing E-learning Statistics for 2020," TechJury, updated June 30, 2020, https://techjury.net/blog/elearning-statistics/#gref.

2. "Watch Out for These 3 Trends Disrupting Marketing! (+ How to Fail Proof Your Business)," *Meera Kothand*, https://www.meerakothand.com/top-digital-marketing-trends/.

3. Meera Kothand, *The One Hour Content Plan: The Solopreneur's Guide to a Year's Worth of Blog Post Ideas in 60 Minutes and Creating Content That Hooks and Sells* (self-pub., CreateSpace, 2017), https://www.amazon.com/dp/B074T5ZHP7/.

4. Meera Kothand, *The Profitable Content System: The Entrepreneur's Guide to Creating Wildly Profitable Content without Burnout*

(self-pub., 2019), https://www.amazon.com/dp/B07Y3SVRF2/.

5. Meera Kothand, *The Blog Startup: Proven Strategies to Launch Smart and Exponentially Grow Your Audience, Brand, and Income without Losing Your Sanity or Crying Bucketloads of Tears* (self-pub., 2020), https://www.amazon.com/dp/B083ZP3PKF.

6. "You Don't Need to Create a Course. Here Are 10 Other Digital Products That Make Bank," *Meera Kothand*, https://www.meerakothand.com/digital-product-ideas/.

7. Meera Kothand, "7 Step Online Course Creation Secret," Meera Kothand, November 25, 2020, YouTube video, 14:36, https://youtu.be/_pbZm_Rxi8Y.

8. Eugene M. Schwartz, *Breakthrough Advertising* (Titans Marketing), https://breakthroughadvertisingbook.com.

9. Meera Kothand, "How to Create & Launch an Online Course That Sells (EVERY.SINGLE.

TIME)," Meera Kothand, November 23, 2020, YouTube video, 14:47, https://youtu.be/WY-BuDkH_r98.

9. Robert French, "If it walks like a duck and quacks like a duck... The Turing Test, Intelligence and Consciousness," ResearchGate, January 2009, https://www.researchgate.net/publication/228825529_If_it_walks_like_a_duck_and_quacks_like_a_duck_The_Turing_Test_Intelligence_and_Consciousness.

10. "How to Survive Your First Opt-in Freebie & Be Successful At It" *Meera Kothand, https://www.meerakothand.com/what-opt-in-freebie-to-create/.*

11. "How To Write Your First Email Sequence," *Meera Kothand*, https://www.meerakothand.com/how-to-write-email-sequence/.

13. Meera Kothand, *300 Email Marketing Tips: Critical Advice and Strategy to Turn Subscribers into Buyers & Grow a Six-Figure*

Business with Email (self-pub., 2019), https://www.amazon.com/dp/B07RXL7NQC.

14. Brian Carroll, *Lead Generation for the Complex Sale* (New York: McGraw-Hill Education, 2006), https://www.amazon.com/Lead-Generation-Complex-Sale-Quantity/dp/0071458972.

Printed in Dunstable, United Kingdom